SMART

OBJECTIVE SETTING
FOR MANAGERS:
A ROADMAP

IRIAL O'FARRELL

First published in USA by
Evolution Consulting, 2020
Dublin, Ireland

ISBN: 978-1-8380731-1-4 (Paperback)

Printed in the USA by Kindle Direct Publishing, Seattle, Washington, USA

Cover Design by 100Covers.com
Interior Design by FormattedBooks.com

OTHER BOOKS BY THIS AUTHOR

Values—Not Just for the Office Wall Plaque:
How Personal and Company Values Intersect

DEDICATION

To Rose, for always being there for me.

YOUR FREE GIFT

While the ideas in this book should sit comfortably with your own organisation's performance-management templates, it's always nice to use a template designed especially for the content rather than trying to figure out the connections.

Go to http://bit.ly/SMARTFreeGifts to choose your free gift:

SMART Objective Setting Meeting Preparation Template
Performance Issues Driver Analysis Template
Manager's Performance Mindset Worksheet
Prompts for You Worksheet

CONTENTS

SUMMARY TABLES

SUMMARY OF SMART OBJECTIVE EXAMPLES

Objective Number	Description	Chapter
1	Do the Dishes	2
2	Run SAP Project (Project X)	3
3	Complete SMART Objectives Book	3
4	SAP Project Revised	3
5	SAP Procurement Project	4
6	Annual Project Volumes	5
7	Learning Procurement Project Process	5
8	Learning Procurement Project Process Revised	5
9	Active Retention of Talent	5
10	SAP Implementation Year 1	6
11	Developing Project Management Skills	7
12	Developing Project Management Skills Revised	7
13	Effective Stakeholder Management	8
14	Communication Skills	8
15	Internal Profile Building	8
16	Internal Profile Building Revised	8
17	Increase Meeting Effectiveness	11

SUMMARY OF TABLES

Table Number	Description	Chapter
1	Sensing vs. Intuition Spectrum	3
2	Categorisation of Objective Drivers	4
3	Sample Procurement Project Categorisation	5
4	Finance Team's SAP project Timeline & Objectives	6
5	Support Types and Examples	7
6	Roadmap Options for Developing Stakeholder Management Skills	8
7	Structure for Designing a Development Objective	8

SUMMARY OF FIGURES

Figure Number	Description	Chapter
1	Partial Organisation Chart for Company 1	Introduction
2	Organisation Chart for Jenny's Team	1
3	Organisation Chart for Chris' Team	4
4	Competency—Autonomy— Relatedness Triangle	9
5	Energy Preferences on a Good Day and Bad Day	Appendix 1
6	Influencing Each of the Colour Preferences	Appendix 1

INTRODUCTION

Since my very first job in Sydney, Australia, I've been fascinated with management and how to match the performance needs of the business with individuals' performance. This has led me on a journey of exploration that has touched on management, personal leadership, organisational leadership, strategy and organisational design, not to mention coaching, training and facilitation.

I have managed both teams and functions and developed others to manage and lead. In my 20 years of experience, a common challenge I've seen managers struggle with is how to set relevant and helpful objectives that make a real difference to their team's performance.

Most managers have heard of the objective-setting acronym of SMART, which stands for:

S—Specific: High-level description of goal to be achieved
M—Measurable: Explains how successfully achieving this goal will be measured
A—Attainable: Considers whether it is possible to achieve this goal
R—Relevant or Realistic: Explains why achieving the goal matters (relevant) or what can realistically be achieved. We will use Relevant in this book
T—Timeframe: Indicates by when the goal should be achieved

When mentioned, SMART often generates a negative response. Digging a bit deeper into managers' concerns, a general sentiment is that while SMART is fine for metric-driven objectives such as "answering X calls in a day" or "producing three programmes with less than Y bugs per programme," they are less useful for softer elements of a role, such as dealing with improving a person's interpersonal skills or generating new ideas. In effect, the general sense is that, while SMART might be somewhat useful for tangible *WHAT* objectives, it is less useful for behavioural *HOW* objectives.

Using the tool with a slightly different approach to the generally accepted way, I have found SMART extremely helpful in setting out effective objectives that really get to the core of performance while setting out a plan to achieve the objective. What I have noticed is that, in discussing and including a plan, the likelihood of the objective being achieved increases, resulting in performance being improved and/or competence developed.

To ensure it wasn't just me that felt managers struggle with objective setting, I asked a group of coaches, HR professionals and executives the following question:

> *In your opinion, what do managers struggle with the most when*
> *setting SMART objectives for their team members?*

The top three answers* were:

1. Lack of training in how to use SMART—30%
2. What to measure—30%
3. Lack of clarity around objectives—17%

Appreciating it is a small sample size, their responses confirmed that (1) it's not just me who recognises that managers struggle with setting SMART objectives and (2) managers struggle with articulating effective objectives. As managers, our ability to set effective objectives that both develop and stretch our team members has a direct impact on our teams' performance and our managerial performance.

*Based on 23 responses.

WHY DESIGNING EFFECTIVE OBJECTIVES MATTERS

As a people manager, with responsibility for performance management, you're likely to fall into one of two camps: (1) oh, thank goodness, a book that finally explains objective setting and SMART written for me; or (2) why do I need a book about designing objectives and using SMART?

If you find yourself in the second camp, it's important to remember the purpose of management, the management tools available and the benefits that accrue. Objective setting is a tool of management designed to actively develop both the individual's and the team's capability to deliver the outputs and outcomes of the team's purpose in the organisation. Individuals who improve their performance increase their job satisfaction, their career prospects and their contribution to the team's overall performance.

In turn, the team collectively delivers more with less emotional conflict and distraction, thus increasing camaraderie and reducing staff turnover. This frees up the manager to take a higher-level view of the team and its role within the organisation and identify high-profile opportunities that both the manager and the individual members of the team can participate in and benefit from.

By investing time and effort in designing effective performance objectives, everybody wins—you as the manager, the individual, the team, the clients or customers, and the organisation as a whole.

WHY WRITE THIS BOOK?

This book is for anyone who has people management responsibilities (i.e., you conduct their performance reviews and set objectives), from team leader up to head of function and CEO. So that you, your team, and your organisation can tap into the benefits of performance development and improvement, the purpose of this book is to enable you to:

- develop a deeper understanding of objective setting within the context of the job description and business strategy;
- recognise aspects that regularly get in the way and how to avoid them;
- leverage a framework to identify and design effective objectives;
- increase your team members' engagement in achieving their objectives.

APPROACH TO SMART OBJECTIVES

This book sets out my approach to designing effective SMART objectives that increases performance. It is based on my experience, both as a manager and as a coach/trainer working with over 1,000 managers. The approach sets out:

- Natural Limitations of the SMART Model
- Surfacing Drivers behind the Need for Objectives
- Identifying Different Objective Types and Impact on Designing Objectives
- Incorporating Individuals' Perspective
- Understanding of Your Performance Mindset as Manager

As we move through the book, I will share typical struggles managers have with objective setting and SMART, through the use of conversations and examples. We will consider the employees' perspective on objective setting along with typical expectations employees have of managers. As we work through this, you, in your role as manager, will also be invited to explore your mindset on performance development.

Along the way, you will meet Jenny, who manages a team of financial accountants, and her colleague, Chris, who manages the procurement team. They both report into Rob, who manages the finance function. We will also meet Rob's peer, Ryan, IT director, and Lena, who works in a tech company and manages a team of programmers. These are fictional characters working in fictional companies, but their performance challenges represent examples of common real-life performance and developmental issues managers face every day. Figure 1 sets out a partial organisation chart of Rob and Ryan's company.

Figure 1: Partial Organisation Chart of Company 1

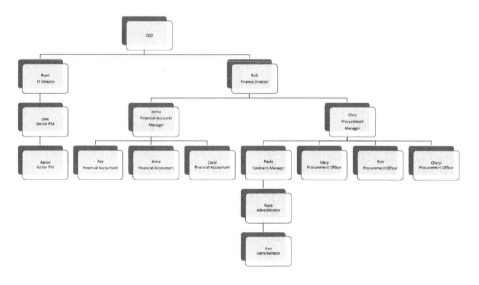

The dialogue shared in the book represents the typical conversations that arise in my Objective-Setting workshops and I have also shared one or two of my all-time favourite incidents that happened, which I hope will be of benefit to you.

The contents of this book complement any specific performance-management process in situ in your own organisation as its focus is on the skills and mindset of objective setting.

SCOPE OF BOOK

This book focuses on objective setting and does not seek to touch on other elements of the performance-management process, e.g. giving effective feedback. I have done this intentionally, to clearly differentiate between the process of setting objectives and evaluating performance. While there are clearly overlaps and dependencies, I find that when I am introducing a new performance-management process, we inevitably draw a line under the old method and start the new process afresh, at the objective-setting stage.

"Drawing a line under the old method" translates to "allowing the managers to evaluate performance in whatever way they have been doing it while recognising that the new performance process will be used for objective setting and future performance evaluation." In effect, the introduction of a new performance-management process starts with the objective-setting process. The quality of the objectives set has a huge bearing on the effectiveness of a performance-management system, which is why this book focuses on the objective-setting stage of performance management.

The other reason is that managers are busy people and for many of them information is best shared when they see the immediate need for it. Explaining how to give effective feedback when they're focused on setting objectives is likely to be a waste of their time as they're not going to need that information for at least three months, if not longer. They won't remember it. They're only really going to focus on the skills around effective feedback when they recognise that they're about to use that information. However, the book does link to why clarifying points during objective setting makes life a lot easier during evaluation and feedback.

While a performance-management process is broader than just the objective setting, i.e. it includes elements such as stages and timings around the organisation's performance-management process, templates, frameworks such as Behavioural Competencies or Role Dimensions, the core management skill of objective setting is both a key competency in all performance-management systems and a key driver of performance success.

Future books will focus on the skills and process of evaluating performance and giving effective feedback, developing high-performance teams, dealing with chronic underperformance, how we can re-imagine and design performance processes, and how to effectively cascade strategy throughout an organisation, aligned with team objectives.

CAPTURING YOUR CURRENT MANAGER'S PERFORMANCE MINDSET

One of the key components to success, in managing performance and developing a team, is the manager's mindset towards performance. We will explore this topic later in the book. In preparation for that section, I invite you to note down your answers to the following questions (click here or go to http://bit.ly/ SMARTFreeGifts, to access your free gift—Manager's Performance Mindset worksheet—or use a blank sheet of paper):

- What value do you see in objective setting? If no value, what are your reasons?
- What assumptions and beliefs do you have around the objective-setting process?
- Where do you think these assumptions* and beliefs** have come from?
- In relation to the objective-setting process, what expectations*** do you have of:
  ○ You, as manager?
  ○ The employee?
  ○ HR?
  ○ Executive team?
  ○ Organisation as a whole?
- For each group above, are these expectations realistic and appropriate?
- In what ways are these assumptions and expectations currently of use to you?
- In what ways are these assumptions and expectations no longer of use to you?

Keep your answers somewhere safe and we will return to them later in the book. I hope that you find the book insightful, that your confidence in setting effective objectives increases, and that you reap the performance improvements within your team.

At the end of each chapter, along with a Summary, there is a Prompts for You section. This outlines some prompts as to how you can apply the chapter's content to your own team's situation. To keep your answers in one place, if you haven't done so already, please feel free to download your free Prompts for You Worksheet by clicking here or going to http://bit.ly/SMARTFreeGifts.

*Assumptions:	Thinking something is true or in place without questioning it or checking whether it is true or not, often without recognising we are making the assumption in the first place.
**Beliefs:	Certain that something is true or exists, often without proof. Beliefs are often subconscious.
***Expectations:	Ways you think things will happen, e.g. how events will unfold, how a person will act, etc.

CHAPTER 1

Linking Job Descriptions and Objectives

Here's a question I regularly pose to mangers:

What's the connection between a Job Description and Objectives?

I'm usually deafened by the silence as they ponder the question and look a little stumped. We rarely step back and think about it, and yet I know from talking to over 1,000 managers that they often struggle with the link between these two tools.

The answer that eventually emerges recognises that the job description sets out the general areas of responsibility and the level of that responsibility (i.e. doing the work, reviewing the work or ensuring the work is done), the types of tasks the employee is expected to do and the knowledge, skills and sometimes the behavioural competencies that are required to succeed in the role. It provides a general sense of what the role entails.

Objectives, on the other hand, set out actual outputs and/or outcomes that need to be delivered in a defined time period. Depending on the role, objectives may identify specific projects to be delivered, as part of the role, name specific client accounts to manage, or they may be in addition to the general responsibilities of the role.

1

Let's look at an example of a job description and related objectives that might be assigned:

FINANCIAL ACCOUNTANT JOB DESCRIPTION

The role will cover all areas of financial management, from the production of monthly management accounts and resolving variances to forecasting, budgeting and project work.

KEY RESPONSIBILITIES INCLUDE:

- Monthly management account preparation
- Production of financial projections
- Production of cash flow forecasts
- Management of account payable and account receivable processes
- Management of all payroll requirements
- Monitoring and advising on operational profitability, for assigned units
- Assisting in annual audit process
- Ensuring all finance-related IT systems are correctly implemented and used
- Implementing internal audit procedures

REQUIREMENTS:

- Qualified accountant
- PQE 2 years minimum

PURPOSE OF JOB DESCRIPTIONS

As we can see from the Financial Accountant example, job descriptions give a fairly general description of the type of work the successful candidate will be doing. It sets out the areas of responsibility and the implied work that is involved. For example, it implies all the work required to prepare the monthly management accounts and cash flow forecasts, as per the company's defined processes. However, what it doesn't include is which specific accounts the incumbent is responsible for, just that these tasks will be their responsibility to complete. There could be 10 people doing this same role, so the job description can't be so specific as to name which accounts.

In effect, behind a job description sit lots of processes, expected standards, timeframes etc., all to be learnt by everyone in this role. For example, someone new to this role will need to learn this company's specific process for how they prepare and produce financial statements. Most likely, there is an accounting software package, such as SAP or SAGE, which needs to be learnt. Then there is the volume of work that is expected to be delivered by certain deadlines. It is also likely that there are different levels of complexity in accounts—some straightforward, others more complex—requiring additional knowledge. None of these aspects are mentioned in the job description.

As we can see from the job description, some line items are more ambiguous and don't necessarily have formal processes to guide them. Let's take the example of the responsibility for ensuring that all finance-related IT systems are correctly implemented and used. Does this imply the need for on-the-job training skills? Does it mean there is an issue with how the current IT system is being used? Is it implying that supporting the need to implement any future IT changes falls within the remit of this role?

The job description doesn't specify. All it says is that "ensures all finance-related IT systems are correctly implemented and used" falls into the responsibilities of this role. There might be one person in this role or there might be 20 people in this role, all of whom share the responsibility. It's fair to conclude that job descriptions give a broad, generic overview of the areas of responsibility and imply some of the processes required to succeed in the role.

As we move up the levels in an organisation, there is a direct correlation between seniority and job description ambiguity. These job descriptions tend to make great use of words such as "managing" and "responsible for" while providing fewer specifics. Unlike with technical aspects, which tend to be supported by written processes and procedures, many organisations have few or no formal management processes in place. This lack of formal management processes further increases the ambiguity of what is expected to deliver the responsibilities outlined in these job descriptions.

In summary, a job description provides a general overview of the type of work and responsibilities an incumbent in the role is expected to deliver.

PURPOSE OF OBJECTIVES

Objectives, on the other hand, set out specific outputs or outcomes the person in this role needs to effectively deliver during a certain period. They are tailored to the person within the role.

Let me introduce Jenny and her team of three financial accountants, one of two finance teams that sit in the finance function, along with the procurement team and the financial controller. These teams report into Rob, the finance director. Jenny's team consists of Ray, Anna and Carol, as shown in Figure 2: Organisation Chart of Jenny's Team.

Figure 2: Organisation Chart for Jenny's Team

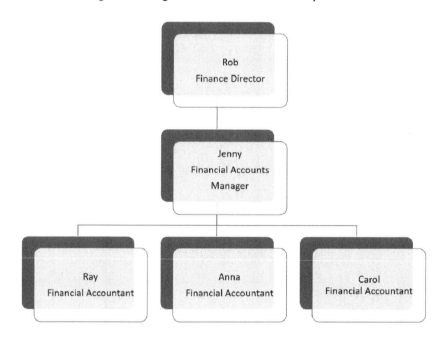

OBJECTIVE TYPES

Jenny needs to set objectives for her team, but what types of objectives can be set? There are internal functional objectives that support the day-to-day running and improvement of the function and give more specific direction to the job description. There are broader, organisational objectives that support the delivery of the business strategy. Finally, there are developmental objectives, which focus on the incumbent developing and/or enhancing their skills, thereby enhancing their performance within their role. In summary, there are three broad categories of objectives:

- Role Specific
- Business Aligned
- Developmental

Let's look at some examples of what these different types of objectives might look like and how they relate to the financial accountant job description.

ROLE-SPECIFIC OBJECTIVES

Ray started off in the accounts payable team. Having earned his accounting qualification two years ago, he moved into Jenny's team and has been working on preparing the various outputs (monthly management accounts, profitability, etc.) for three business units—US Retail, US eCommerce, and US Operations. The team has been fairly stable since Ray joined, so Jenny figures movement of some sort (e.g., departure, promotion, secondment) is likely to be on the horizon. To ensure continuity and succession planning, she has identified that Ray needs to get up to speed on more complex business units, so Jenny sets him an objective to take over responsibility for the Europe, Middle East and Africa (EMEA) retail, eCommerce and distribution business units.

This objective is in keeping with Ray's job description, which calls out the outputs but doesn't name the business units, and it is also in line with the job's responsibilities.

So, one purpose of objective setting is to provide specific direction on what the individual is responsible for during the performance period, within the context of all aspects of the role being performed. The implication here is that, once Ray has taken over the management of the EMEA business units, he will continue to do so, until they are reassigned to someone else. His objective is really to master the nuances of these business units and deliver each account's outputs. The standards and the timeframes are likely to remain the same as they are likely to be the same across all the business units. Should they differ, this objective would also include understanding the new standards and timeframes and delivering them accordingly.

BUSINESS ALIGNMENT OBJECTIVES

Another purpose of objective setting is to ensure that the specifics within a role are aligned to the functional strategy, business and/or corporate strategy or annual business plan. As it happens, Jenny's company has determined that it needs greater real-time insight into its sales revenue and costs so that the executive team can make more informed and timely decisions. To enable this, they've decided to install SAP across the whole organisation.

The finance function has been tasked with both sourcing the right SAP consultants, to assist with implementation across the organisation, and ensuring SAP is implemented correctly within the finance function. Rob, the finance director, assigns the sourcing element of the project to the procurement team and assigns the implementation element to all teams within Finance. Jenny, in turn, needs to consider how her team is going to deliver their assigned responsibilities.

Having weighed up the pros and cons of how best to divide out the responsibilities and tasks, and having considered the developmental needs of each team member, Jenny decides to assign responsibility to manage the implementation project to one person, e.g. Ray, while setting Carol and Anna an objective that supports the implementation of SAP, by assigning certain tasks from the team's project implementation plan to each of them. Ray has been charged with creating and managing the project plan, with related milestones, tasks, outputs, etc., while Carol and Anna will be charged with delivering assigned tasks from the project plan, once available.

In this case, the above objective aligns Ray's, Carol's and Anna's objectives with the overall business need to implement SAP while having slightly different objectives. This is an example of an objective being aligned with the company's business or strategic objectives.

Taking a look at the job description, we can see that it allows for the financial accountant role to be responsible for ensuring the implementation and appropriate application of the IT system while the objectives set out specifically what needs to happen to migrate their IT finance system to SAP. Again, once the project element of the objective, "to implement and embed SAP", is achieved, the ongoing use of SAP to deliver the role outputs is implied as that will be the IT system of choice in place to deliver the outputs.

DEVELOPMENTAL OBJECTIVES

A third purpose of objective setting is to develop and enhance the knowledge, skills and competence required to deliver the role successfully. When a person is new to a role, they need to learn the various aspects of the role, such as tasks, context, outputs, standards, volumes, etc. Once they have learnt the basics, they can focus on mastering the nuances of the role. Eventually, they start stretching themselves, to gain new skills, experience and understanding, which, in turn, helps their career progression.

As Ray has a couple of years of experience, he already knows the system, processes, required standards and volumes, workflows etc. While his move to working with the EMEA business units is role specific (i.e., it's part of his job description), it is also developmental in that he will need to learn the nuances of these business lines and the individual players in these business units. For example, he'll need to figure out what's important to these business units, what does and doesn't work in their work cultures, etc. So this objective is both role specific and developmental.

The important thing with a developmental objective is determining what training and support Ray will need. If there are no particular quirks with the required outputs, then it's just a case of understanding the nuances of the different players, which is within Ray's control to figure out. A quick 10–15-minute chat with the person currently working with those business units would also give Ray a steer in the right direction.

If these business units are more complex or in different business lines, there may be specific knowledge or skills required to successfully manage these accounts. For example, as Ray is moving from looking after business units all based in one country, i.e., the USA, to looking after business units based in several jurisdictions, i.e., EMEA, Ray will need to get his head around all the numerous differences, both in terms of accounting and reporting. In this case, it is unlikely that it's in Ray's control to figure out what is different, so some sort of training session would be prudent. Personally, I'd hate to be the manager having to explain that my financial accountant didn't understand the nuanced differences between GAAP and international accounting rules and that's why we've a large outstanding tax bill to pay.

While the change in Ray's responsibility to manage a different set of business units can be considered an example of a developmental objective, it is really an example of a *WHAT* developmental objective. In this case, it is developing Ray's technical understanding and experience by assigning him responsibility for the EMEA business units. As a result of this *WHAT* developmental objective, he will expand his technical knowledge and expertise within the context of his role.

In my experience, setting a SMART objective for a *what* objective is relatively straightforward and managers typically do a good job of setting these types of objectives. However, it's not usually an individual's technical *what* abilities that drive the manager to distraction, it is the softer, *how* they go about applying their technical abilities that managers often struggle with; for example, *how* a person communicates or *how* they problem solve or *how* they influence others. This type of development is often referred to as a *HOW* or behavioural objective.

In Ray's case, Jenny has noticed that he is very good at the technical aspects of his role; however, he sometimes trips himself up by not explaining and engaging his business unit stakeholders on a timely basis. She's noticed that there have been several times when silly things have escalated unnecessarily, which really isn't helping Ray's reputation, the team's or Jenny's.

Along with the *what* developmental objective of managing the EMEA business units, Jenny recognises that Ray also needs to develop his stakeholder management capabilities. Looking back to the job description, we can see that stakeholder management capabilities aren't clearly called out anywhere. However, as Ray is responsible for "monitoring and advising on operational profitability" for his assigned units, his poor stakeholder management skills are getting in his way of successfully doing this. So, Jenny is also going to set Ray a *HOW* developmental objective, focused on developing his stakeholder management skills.

CHAPTER SUMMARY

The purpose of a job description is to paint a picture of the broad responsibilities of a role. By definition, a job description can't get too specific. On the other hand, the purpose of setting objectives is to provide individual direction to employees regarding what they need to focus on and deliver during a set period, within the context of delivering their role and supporting the business strategy.

There are three broad purposes of objective setting:

1. Provide specific direction on what the individual is responsible for within the context of their role being performed
2. Ensure aspects within a role are aligned to the functional or business strategy
3. Develop knowledge, skills, and competence to deliver the current role or future role

To support the purposes of objective setting, there are four types of objectives:

-   Role-specific: to provide specific direction within the role, e.g. designated clients, identified processes
-   Business-aligned: to deliver explicit aspects of the business strategy so that the strategic goals are realised in time
-   Technical "What" developmental: to develop selected capabilities and skills needed to deliver the role effectively
-   Behavioural "How" developmental: to develop the softer, interpersonal capabilities and skills required to succeed in the role

PROMPTS FOR YOU:

For one member of your team, identify a possible objective from each objective type.

C H A P T E R   2

The Catch with SMART

Having looked at the relationship between Job Description and Objectives, as managers, how do we approach the process of setting objectives? Following on from Chapter 1, Jenny has identified three solid objectives for Ray to focus on for the coming period:

–   Be responsible for various outputs for EMEA business units [role specific]
–   Project manage SAP implementation project for the team [business-aligned]
–   Enhance stakeholder management skills [behavioural development]

Jenny feels that succeeding in these three objectives will really boost both Ray's and the team's performance in the short-term while enhancing Ray's career prospects in the longer-term. So, what does Jenny need to do now?

Having identified his objectives, Jenny could just leave it until she meets with Ray and discuss the objectives with him then. However, as we will see, Jenny's understanding of what each of these objectives means and how they will be evaluated might be the same as Ray's understanding or, much more likely, could be wildly different. Enter the SMART model, which, as we saw in the Introduction, stands for:

S   Specific
M   Measurable
A   Attainable
R   Relevant*
T   Timeframe

*Some people use the word Realistic rather than Relevant. As Realistic is very closely aligned with Attainable, I prefer to use Relevant to allow for a link between the objective and why it matters.

Using SMART has long been accepted as the most effective way for setting out objectives. However, many managers dislike SMART, so much so that I usually expect a groan or two when I mention the acronym. What I have noticed is that many managers struggle to use SMART in any useful way, particularly when it comes to behavioural, *how* objectives. I find that once they've gone through my SMART Objective Setting workshop, they are much clearer on how to use it, both with the *WHAT* and the *HOW* objectives, and are much more positive about using SMART.

At the start of the workshop, having checked that participants know what SMART stands for, and regardless of my audience, I ask the group if the following objective is SMART:

"I'm going out, can you do the dishes?"

The conversation usually runs something like this:

Them: No, there's no timeframe.
Me: Okay then, I'll rephrase: I'm going out; I'll be back in an hour. Can you have the dishes done?

Them: Yeah, that's SMART.
Me: Is it?

Them: Eh, yeah, it's SMART. You have the specific and the measurable and the timeframe. The relevant and attainable are both fine.
Me: So, is it SMART?

Them: Yes.
Me: You're sure?

Them: Yep, we're sure.
Me: Okay, so hands up; whose idea of doing the dishes is "washing the dishes and letting them drip-dry on the counter"?

The bigger the group, the more likely you are to get a couple of people putting their hands up.

Me: So, whose idea of doing the dishes is "washing the dishes and drying them"?

Usually, a few hands go up.

Me: Whose idea of doing the dishes is "washing and drying them and putting them away"?

The majority of hands go up for this one, often along with one or two hands from the previous group with "Oh, that's what I meant" or "Oh, that's what I thought you meant" type comments.

Me: Whose idea is "washing, drying and putting away the dishes and wiping down the counters"?

Usually, the rest of the hands go up on this one, with everyone else in the room feeling like they've been shamed by their lack of cleaning prowess. This one is often accompanied by some knowing laughs, as they now understand why they constantly end up in arguments at home about the dishes being "done".

In one session, one person didn't put up their hand so I asked them why, to which they replied, "Oh, my idea of doing the dishes is all of the above and sweeping the floors." Upon recovering from my chastisement, I added this option into workshops and, yes, occasionally it does get selected.

One of my all-time favourite responses to this exercise was an exclamation of, "Oh, you want the kitchen cleaned." We all fell around the place laughing at the implied nuanced difference between the phrases "doing the dishes" and "cleaning the kitchen". To this person, there was clearly a difference. To the rest of us, they were two ways of saying the same thing.

Once the laughing has settled down, I highlight that SMART can be very effective in setting out and framing an objective. However, a natural constraint exists when using SMART between two people. So, care needs to be taken in clearly constructing an objective and ensuring a common understanding between both parties. Otherwise, issues will arise due to differences in expectations. If someone initially selected the second dishes option and then changed it to the third option, I highlight the point that, if the manager isn't clear on what is expected, how can the employee be clear?

I use this example because, regardless of level, everyone can understand and relate to it and it beautifully highlights that, for such a simple task, there are five or six different ways it can be interpreted while *looking* like a SMART objective. Here's how many managers would instinctively set out this objective, using SMART and prior to attending the workshop:

SMART Objective 1: Do the Dishes

SPECIFIC:	Do the dishes
MEASURABLE:	Dishes are done
ATTAINABLE:	Yes
RELEVANT:	Dishes need to be done to be available for next meal
TIMEFRAME:	1 hour

As we saw above, the expectations around "dishes are done" can vary widely and assuming that both parties have the same understanding of what "dishes are done" means is a recipe for disaster. For example, if my expectation is that they'll be washed, dried, put away and the counters wiped down, I'm not going to be very happy when I arrive home and they're drip-drying on the counter with the counters all dirty.

As a manager, the last thing you want is to set an objective and assume there's a shared understanding of how the objective's success will be evaluated, only to find out in six or twelve months' time, at the review meeting, that you thought the objective was half delivered while the employee thought they nailed it.

The dishes example very neatly highlights the catch with using SMART. Most of the literature for SMART assumes that it is the individual setting the goal for themselves, e.g. increase your income, lose 10 lbs. There's not as much literature for using SMART as a tool for joint goal setting as part of Performance Management and Development. The assumption is that there is no difference in using the tool for yourself as using it in conjunction with another person. However, as we saw with even a very simple task, it takes two to tango and different assumptions can lead to broken toes. Similarly, differing assumptions and expectations can doom objectives from the very start and lead to emotional responses, conflict, withdrawal, and disengagement. The more complex the objectives, the more compounded these negative impacts can become. Over time, organisations end up with increased costs associated with underperformance, lack of co-operation, higher employee turnover, and costs of paying twice for the same work to be done or to replace the knowledge and skills lost.

Understanding the catch, and implementing strategies to overcome it, can turn SMART into a very powerful management tool for objective setting and staff development. Many managers have a good idea of how their employees need to develop but struggle with converting them into tangible, SMART objectives. Having worked through some of these situations with them during workshops, managers see how it is possible to develop robust objectives, even on topics as nebulous as Building Trust.

As part of this book, we will deconstruct the SMART tool while layering in an understanding of how humans work, so that managers understand how to use SMART effectively, both in conjunction with another person and with different objective types and performance levels. This will provide a deeper understanding of objective setting while also understanding how the process can easily be undermined.

As we will see, effectively using SMART requires upfront preparation and effort by the manager, prior to the objective-setting meeting, along with a constructive, two-way conversation during the objective-setting meeting. Investing time upfront results in a better-framed objective and increased clarity and agreement on a route to deliver it, what a successful outcome looks like, and the support required to achieve it. The payoff for the manager is a reduction in conflict and wasted emotional energy six or twelve months down the line and an increase in the likelihood of improved performance, by the individual and the team.

CHAPTER SUMMARY

SMART is a tried and tested tool to set out and frame objectives. However, much of the literature focuses on using SMART to set one's own goals. When using it to set objectives with another person, it is very easy for assumptions to arise around the purpose of the objective, what success will look like, how to approach achieving the objective, and constraints and support.

Care needs to be taken when using SMART with another person. Time and effort need to be invested in planning the SMART objective-setting process in order to uncover hidden assumptions and expectations and prevent problems down the road.

A well-designed and framed SMART objective can increase employee buy-in and engagement, resulting in increased competence, confidence and capability; in turn resulting in better performance.

PROMPTS FOR YOU:

Think about an individual you will be setting objectives for and identify a relevant objective for them or think about an objective you set for them during the last objective-setting cycle. Answer the following questions:

- What assumptions are you making about this individual in relation to this objective?
- What impact do these assumptions have on your approach to setting this objective?
- For negative impacts, what could you do to reduce the impact of these assumptions?

CHAPTER 3

Smart Use of SMART

We saw from the previous chapter that SMART stands for:

S Specific
M Measurable
A Attainable
R Relevant or realistic
T Time bound

We know that the theory of SMART is that if we are more specific about defining our goals, we are more likely to achieve our goals. From experience, we sense that objective setting can often become a cut-and-paste exercise HR makes us do. We also saw how easy it is for unsurfaced assumptions and expectations to scupper objective success when setting objectives with another person.

Returning to Jenny and Ray, who we met in Chapter 1, let's take a closer look at the SAP project as laid out below:

SMART Objective 2: Run SAP (Project X) Project

SPECIFIC: Run SAP project (project X)
MEASURABLE: Project delivered on time and on budget
ATTAINABLE: Yes

Relevant: Yes
Timeframe: As per project plan

We can see that Jenny has filled in answers for each of the letters of the SMART acronym, so it must be SMART, right? Just like the dishes example, we could justifiably answer this question as follows:

- *It mentions the SAP project, so it's specific.*
- *The project will have outputs, budgets, tasks, milestones, and timeframes, so we can say it's measurable as the project will define the outputs and budgets so that success can be measured by delivery of them.*
- *It should be attainable as it is a bone fide strategic project that has been approved and will be monitored by the executive team.*
- *It feeds into the business strategy plan, so it's relevant.*
- *Finally, since the project plan will outline the timeframe for delivery, we automatically have timeframes defined.*
- *In conclusion, yep—this is a SMART objective.*

While we can justify that this is a SMART objective, it's not a particularly informative objective. It's a great example of running through the motions of a SMART objective. It has an "I'm not too sure what I'm supposed to put in under each of these letters" feel to it. It also completely misses the point.

If "running projects" was the purpose of Ray's role, it would be even less useful as it would mean that every project would need to be set out as an objective, even though delivering projects is the purpose of the role, and every time a project changed or was cancelled or reassigned, the objectives would need to be updated to reflect this, rendering the process impractical as we're all very busy. We will revisit this point in Chapter 5.

More importantly, I've seen many managers and employees set these types of objectives at the beginning of the year and end up very frustrated at review time, six or 12 months later. One party, often the employee, thinks the objective has either been achieved or became impossible to deliver on, while the other party, often the manager, thinks it's maybe half done or fails to recognise that the project couldn't be delivered for reasons outside of the employee's control.

As we saw with the straightforward dishes example, many things can go astray in two people's understanding of an objective. As illustrated in Chapter

2, an implicit assumption with the theory and literature for SMART objective setting is that the person *setting* the goal is also the person *doing* the goal.

For example, when I'm setting a goal for myself, I know, or have a sense of, what I mean in relation to what the goal is intended to achieve, what the measure of success looks like to me, what needs to be done during the time-frame and the specific steps that I need to do in order to deliver the objective. I know these things because it's my goal and I am setting it for me. For example, I could set out the following SMART objective:

SMART Objective 3: Complete SMART Objectives Book

SPECIFIC: Complete the book on SMART Objectives
MEASURABLE: Book available for purchase
ATTAINABLE: Yes
RELEVANT: Build profile as experienced executive coach and trainer
TIMEFRAME: 1st September, 2020

On the surface of it, we can both agree that this is a tangible SMART goal. As it's *my* SMART goal, I know exactly what I mean by it. The question is would you interpret it in the same way? In reality, I know that it's not just about having the book up on Amazon and Kindle; it's also about ensuring that it is selling. So, I know that the measurable is really about the book generating sales, but I'm using the "Book available for purchase" as a proxy for the book selling.

I also know that implied in the timeframe of 1st September is a whole project plan of tasks to be achieved, such as:

- Write first draft
- Review first draft and edit into second draft
- Decide name and get cover designed
- Identify any images/graphs required and get them ready
- Figure out all elements required for an eBook on different ereaders and ensure they're all prepared
- Figure out all elements required for an audio book format
- Decide on final price for each book format
- Proofread final draft
- Format correctly for each distribution channel

- Upload material onto Amazon, Kindle and other paperback and eBook distributors
- Create marketing plan
- Execute marketing plan

Since it's my objective, I don't really need to outline all the tasks and milestones that need to be done to achieve this objective. I can just write down a target date, in this case September 1st, and in my head I have an idea of the various different aspects that need to be completed by then.

If I set the above objective for you, would you know that all these aspects were implied? I know what *I* mean, but do *you* know what *I* mean? As we saw with the dishes, this is where the theory of SMART starts to become slightly unstuck, using it to set objectives with someone else.

USING SMART WITH EMPLOYEES

When it comes to managing and developing our teams' performance, how do we *really* need to use SMART? As managers, when we use SMART, a better way to think about it is as a tool to create the space to have a two-way conversation about surfacing the assumptions and expectations of both parties and closing the gaps between them. If I was to set the above objective with an employee, I would use SMART to generate a conversation to ensure that they definitely twig that the objective is about the book being both available and *selling,* rather than not knowing what their assumptions are and perhaps allowing them to assume that once the book is available it's mission accomplished.

You might laugh and say, *"Of course* they would know that it's about *selling* the book and not *just* having it available," but I've worked with numerous managers that start off stating the objective they want to set is X, only to figure out, through my approach to SMART objective setting, that the objective is actual Y. If the manager struggles to articulate and isolate what the objective actually is, how can the employee know what it actually means?

IMPACT OF PERSONALITY PREFERENCES ON EXPECTATIONS

Another perspective on why it's important to clearly articulate expectations comes from personality models such as Insights Discovery® and Myers-Briggs. Based on the work of Carl Jung's theories, both of these models identify the concept of Sensing vs. Intuition, a spectrum indicating how different people receive and process new information. A preference for Sensing indicates a person receives and processes information in a very practical, literal way. A person with a preference for Intuition is more likely to process information in a more abstract, conceptual way. Typical words used to describe the two ends of the Sensing—Intuition spectrum are shown in Table 1.

Table 1: Sensing vs. Intuition Spectrum

SENSING	INTUITION
Specific	General
Present-focused	Future-focused
Practical	Conceptual
Factual	Theoretical
Literal	Metaphorical
Step-by-step	Evolving
Realistic	Imaginative

Research evidence from Insights Discovery® indicates that roughly half the British population is Sensing (50.42%) while the other half (49.58%) is Intuitive. In practice, this translates to roughly half the population is likely to assume that the expectation of an objective is exactly as specified, while the other half is likely to assume that the expectation is the concept of the objective, not the literal interpretation.

Layering in the different approaches to processing of information on top of assumptions and expectations, we can see why setting SMART objectives with an employee is not straightforward and why managers struggle with the objective-setting process. See Appendix 1 for more information on Carl Jung's theories and Insights Discovery's energy preferences.

REAL PURPOSE OF SMART

As already mentioned, I see SMART as a tool that enables the manager to create the space to have a real and detailed discussion with the employee about what an objective really means. This increases the likelihood that both parties will leave the objective-setting process with an agreed understanding of:

- what the objective actually is
- how it should be attained
- what level of support might be needed for it to be achieved
- where that support will come from
- what success will look like
- who is responsible for achieving the goal vs. provision of support

In summary, the real purpose of SMART is that it is a tool to prompt a two-way conversation about what needs to be achieved within the period to ensure that both parties are clear about what the success of those achievements will look like and to identify the implicit boundaries, constraints and supports.

BENEFITS OF USING SMART EFFECTIVELY

If you're thinking that using this approach will initially take you more time and effort to shape more effective objectives, you're right, it will. However, using this approach pays dividends down the road in several ways:

1. Both parties are clear about what the objective actually is and what success really looks like.
2. Both parties have a clear map as to how the objective can be achieved and what support is required.
3. A shared vision of success reduces the conflict that can arise when both parties evaluating the success of an objective have different images of a successful outcome.
4. The process increases the likelihood of the objective being achieved, increasing performance and competence.

There's no point crying over spilt milk and using the performance review meeting to figure out what the successful objective outcome should have looked like is neither the time nor the place. Following this approach, SMART allows that conversation to happen upfront, when designing the objective, making the review meeting a lot less confrontational, which is always a bonus.

DESIGNING A MORE EFFECTIVE SMART OBJECTIVE

Re-examining the objective Jenny set Ray, what might a more effective SMART objective look like?

SMART Objective 4: Original & Revised SAP Project

SMART	ORIGINAL	REVISED
SPECIFIC	Run SAP project	Ensure SAP is implemented within team
MEASURABLE	Project delivered on time and on budget	All team members using SAP with no major issues arising with other functions
ATTAINABLE	Yes	Yes, assuming SAP installed & made available
RELEVANT	Yes	Part of business strategy
TIMEFRAME	As per project plan	**End-Month 1:** Project plan agreed **End-Month 2–5:** Project progress meetings. **End-month 6:** Project implemented, as per project plan

LEARNING POINTS FROM THIS SMART OBJECTIVE

SPECIFIC:

Looking at the two SMART objectives side by side, we can see subtle differences between the two options. The original objective Specific was to run the project, but that's not really the purpose. It's really to ensure that the team are (1) using

SAP and (2) their use of SAP is not causing issues down the line. Again, while we could argue the toss and say that "ensuring SAP is implemented" is part of the project plan, there are likely to be subtle differences in outcomes.

For example, the SAP project plan may well have a task to "train the team on using SAP"; that doesn't automatically mean that the team will start using the system. That will require follow-up, monitoring, coaching, etc. By phrasing it as per the revised objective, all the little subtleties of ensuring each individual is using SAP correctly are captured in a way "Run SAP project" doesn't.

MEASURABLE:

The measurables in both objectives are quite different too. One is only focused on delivering the tasks of the project, as per the agreed timeframes and budget. Ray could easily point to SAP being implemented and everybody on the team having been trained, yet the team's use of SAP could be causing all sorts of problems for the team and other users. Most likely, the outcome Jenny expects is more aligned with the team being able to use the system effectively rather than just the project having been delivered—very subtle differences but enough to cause differences in perceived achievement during the review and frustration that SAP is causing Jenny "noise" from other functions, i.e. grumbles and complaints.

ATTAINABLE:

The original SMART objective implies there are no constraints or barriers to attaining this objective while, in reality, there are. If there are problems with the procurement team finalising the contracts, it will delay this objective. If the IT function runs into problems, again there will be knock-on impacts. If politics rears its ugly head, there will be knock-on impacts. These are outside Ray's control, so holding him to this objective when issues outside his control could render the objective unattainable needs to be acknowledged.

Not acknowledging the knock-on effects of these constraints on the attainability of the objectives may cause unnecessary anxiety. Depending on Ray's seniority, experience, ability to see potential roadblocks and dependencies, beliefs and assertiveness, he may spot these potential issues and raise his concerns. Or he may just sit there, expecting his manager to call these out. If he has spotted them and they haven't been called out, Ray may well walk out of the objective-setting meeting thinking he's doomed before he's already started. Not the best starting point for success.

RELEVANT:

Rather than just acknowledge that the objective is relevant to Ray's role, it can be very helpful to highlight exactly how it is relevant. In this case, the objective links to a high-profile project that supports the achievement of the company's business strategy. Depending on the objective type, i.e. role specific, business strategy or developmental, the specific relevance will change.

While Jenny, as a manager, might feel that this is a waste of time or unnecessary, it's worthwhile remembering that a common complaint from employees is that they don't have a direct line of sight between their job and the company's strategy. According to research undertaken by author and consultant William Schiemann, only 14% of employees understand their company's strategy and direction. By clearly calling out the relevance, it can aid in connecting the individual to the company's strategic objectives.

TIMEFRAME:

Finally, putting some structure around the timeframe expectations (i.e. what should happen, by when) for this objective can be extremely helpful for both sides. As we can see from the two objectives, the first one references the project plan while the second one sets out specific expectations such as "agree a project plan" and "progress meetings".

I always remember a specific incident that occurred when my mother was away and I was put in charge of looking after the house for my dad and me. I had cleaned the kitchen when one of my brothers, who no longer lived in the house but made regular use of it, arrived and made a sandwich. I started to berate him for not having cleaned up after himself prior to eating the sandwich. He argued back that he would do so when he had finished eating. Who knows whether he would or wouldn't have cleaned up but, since I hadn't waited for evidence of him leaving the room without cleaning up, I ended up on the back foot.

I share this story to highlight the point about expectations and the timing of when they should be addressed. I had an expectation that my brother would clean up before eating the sandwich. However, I didn't express it. On the other hand, he thought doing so after eating was just fine and since I didn't express my expectation, he didn't have the opportunity to counter it i.e., tell me he'd do it after he had eaten. The learning, for me, was that I acted on my expectation without either expressing it or waiting to see if the expectation would be met, at a later time.

Likewise, if Jenny has an expectation that the project plan will be laid out, to be discussed and agreed with the team (not an unreasonable assumption, given that she has decided that Ray should run the SAP project and that Carol and Anna will be assigned tasks from the project plan), it is likely Jenny has a time-frame by which she expects this to happen, e.g. by the end of the first month.

If Ray is an "I have it all in my head" type of person or "last-minute merchant" and Jenny doesn't share her expectation around the need for a project plan with him, it is likely that Jenny is going to get very irritated with Ray when he doesn't meet her expectation, and Ray is going to be oblivious to the source of Jenny's irritation while thinking he's doing a great job working away on the tasks.

USING SMART TO CREATE A ROADMAP

Theory of SMART indicates that we include a deadline as to when the goal should be achieved. However, we have seen that when the goal is being agreed by two parties, assumptions can very easily creep in that can lead to differences of opinion, both in terms of what the goal actually means and expectations of how it should be achieved.

Using the Timeframe element of SMART to set out a roadmap of how the goal is expected to be achieved permits a two-way conversation that explores what the goal outcome(s) is really about and how best to approach it. In turn, this exploration creates a more meaningful goal while managing both parties' expectations about what needs to be done, what supports and inputs are required, what constraints might exist and guidance on how to deal with them.

Continuously setting ill-thought-out goals for employees does nobody any favours, neither the employee nor the manager. Creating a roadmap to success increases the likelihood of the goal being achieved as it helps both parties visualise what is involved in achieving it. In turn, a goal achieved develops a more competent and confident employee, a more effective team and a more positive working environment.

SELF-DETERMINATION THEORY OF MOTIVATION

Building competence, exploring and inviting input into how a goal can be achieved, relating the goal to a wider purpose; these are all elements that can tap into a person's intrinsic motivators. We will explore motivating factors and Self-Determination Theory, and ways to connect an individual's motivation to wanting to achieve an objective in more detail in later chapters.

CHAPTER SUMMARY

When using SMART as the basis of designing an objective between two people, it should be used to generate a two-way conversation to surface assumptions, articulate expectations, agree what success looks like and identify potential supports and constraints.

Preparing for and conducting such a conversation takes more time using this approach as compared to a quick "here are your objectives for the period" meeting. While there are no guarantees, the outcomes are more likely to be achieved using this approach so are more rewarding for the employee, the team, the manager and the company as a whole. That sense of achievement builds its own momentum.

As with anything, the more often we practice this approach to SMART objective setting, the quicker and easier it becomes.

PROMPTS FOR YOU:

What benefits do you think can be gained by:

- Defining the outcome of an objective rather than outputs?
- Linking the objective to one of the four objective types, i.e. role-specific, business-aligned, technical competency and behavioural competency?
- Identifying possible constraints of and supports needed when designing an objective?
- Creating a roadmap to objective success?

CHAPTER 4

Assessing Objective Drivers

Before we move on to looking at how to design appropriate SMART objectives for the different objective types in more detail, we first need to consider what the drivers are behind the need for any given objective. Some drivers are very obvious. For example, the driver behind Ray's SAP project objective is clearly the business need to have more real-time data available to better inform decisions. Another clear driver is when someone is new to their role. There is clearly a need to get them trained up on the various tasks and processes of their role.

However, other drivers can be less clear, particularly developmental objectives for someone who has been in their role for a while. For example, what if Ray's objective was for someone whose role was project-based?

Jenny's colleague, Chris, manages the procurement team. He has a team of three procurement officers (Ron, Cheryl and Mary) along with two administrators (Rose and Ken), and a contracts manager (Paula) who manages the administrators, as can be seen in Figure 3: Organisational Chart for Chris' Team. The procurement officer's role is to manage the procurement needs for assigned business units. Typically, this involves delivering several procurement projects throughout the year.

Figure 3: Organisational Chart for Chris' Team

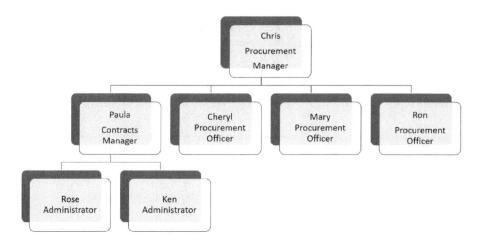

Mary is responsible for the finance function's procurement needs. So, when Chris was assigned the business-aligned objective to secure SAP consultants, he allocated the procurement project to Mary. Chris sets her objective as follows:

SMART Objective 5: SAP Procurement Project

SPECIFIC:	Procure SAP implementation consultancy services
MEASURABLE:	SAP consultancy services contract in place
ATTAINABLE:	Yes, assuming budgetary approval
RELEVANT:	Strategic initiative
TIMEFRAME:	*End-month 1:* tender request document approved and distributed
	End-month 3: evaluate tender responses
	End-month 4: conclude contract with successful candidate

Looking at this, we can all agree that this is definitely a SMART objective. However, it's worthwhile taking a step back and asking ourselves, "What is Chris seeking to achieve with this objective?" This objective, while SMART, is overly specific for someone whose job is to deliver procurement projects. A question for Chris to consider is:

What is driving the need for this performance objective for Mary?

Unlike with Ray, whose SAP project objective was a specific objective to be delivered, while also delivering his daily, weekly, and monthly account outputs for his assigned business units, Mary's role is to deliver a certain number of projects per year. While some projects may be complex and some may be straightforward, her role is to deliver X number of procurement projects and to have Y number of tender contracts in place to be utilised by her assigned business units. So, for Mary, the SAP procurement project is just one of several tenders she will need to manage throughout the year as part of her business-as-usual (BAU) role. So why would Chris specifically call out this objective for Mary?

As it happens, Chris has had several complaints from Mary's assigned business unit stakeholders. The general gist of the complaints is that Mary takes way too long to get the tender out to the supplier tender list and never seems to be available for the tender evaluation meetings. This is slowing the tender process down considerably and is having a knock-on impact on her business units. Rob, the finance director, has also passed a comment or two. Before setting this objective, Chris needs to figure out the drivers behind Mary's performance issue. Some questions he could pose are:

- Is this about volume and timeframes, i.e. does Mary understand the number of projects she should deliver per year or roughly how long each project type should take to be completed? Does she have an idea of roughly how long it should take a typical project from start to finish?
- Is Mary new to project management and needing to upskill on managing projects?
- Is Mary new to the procurement project process and so needing to build up her competency in the procurement process?
- Is it about Mary's approach to running procurement projects, e.g. does Mary need to set out her projects with stages and check-in points?
- Is it about Mary's ability to manage stakeholders' expectations effectively?
- Is it about Mary's time-management skills and ability to juggle several projects?

Each of these questions is seeking to isolate a possible driver behind Mary's performance. By answering the questions, it can help identify what is really happening with her performance. Chris can't definitively know what the drivers are, so he is going to need to discuss and explore this with Mary. However, he can prepare for that discussion by reflecting on the evidence, his experience, his understanding of Mary's performance to date, and the organisational culture. This can help him to identify some of the reasons he feels might be playing into the performance concerns. He can then use those insights as the basis of opening up the conversation with Mary. In short, he doesn't have to have the answers going into the meeting, but he needs to demonstrate some level of management by prompting Mary as to what might be going on with her.

Looking at these possible drivers, we can see that Chris might set very different SMART objectives, depending on the driver(s) behind Mary's performance and behaviour. He decides to categorise the drivers by objective type, as outlined in Table 2:

Table 2: Categorisation of Objective Drivers

OBJECTIVE CATEGORY	DRIVER
ROLE SPECIFIC	SAP procurement project Number of projects per year New to procurement process
BUSINESS STRATEGY	SAP procurement project
TECHNICAL COMPETENCY	New to project management Approach to running procurement projects
BEHAVIOURAL COMPETENCY	Stakeholder management Time management

As we can see, from just one project Chris could end up setting Mary an objective from any of the four objective types, and they would all look quite different. We can also see the importance of understanding the drivers behind the need to set an objective as it is a key requirement in selecting and setting the right objective type that will result in increased performance.

In my experience, identifying the drivers is much harder than it sounds. For example, when I run a SMART Objective Setting workshop with managers, I usually ask for someone to volunteer a real-life objective that they'd like to set for one of their team. Somebody inevitably throws out a suggestion for us to work through. Typically, they'll say they want to set an objective about X, so I capture an initial first cut of the objective. I then facilitate a conversation with the group to explore what the objective is really about. It regularly turns out that the objective isn't quite X. It may be X+ or it may be Y or it may be Z which includes X as a step along the way.

For example, if Chris was in my workshop, he might have suggested the need to develop someone's project management skills (X), which I would note down. The conversation might run something along the lines of:

Me: So, Chris, what's not working about their project-management skills?

Chris: Well, they're taking ages to get from start to finish on their projects.

Me: How do you know this?

Chris: I'm starting to get complaints from the business units.

Me: And are they right? Is the person taking much longer than they should be to finish projects?

Chris: Well, I'm not too sure. Some of the projects they've been working on are particularly complex, so that will inevitably extend the length of the project.

Me: And do the users know this?

Chris: How do you mean?

Me: Well, are those users used to complex projects or have they been used to simpler, shorter projects and don't understand or recognise that the more recent projects are more complex and so will naturally take longer?

Chris: Em, I'm not too sure if the person would have necessarily pointed that out to them. I doubt they are aware that the projects are more complex.

Me: How long has this person been in the role?

Chris: Three years.

Me: Has this ever been an issue before?

Chris: No, not that I'm aware of.

Me: So is this about their project-management skills or their stakehold-er-expectation-management skills?

Chris: Well, now that I think about it, it could be about expectation management.

On the surface of it, it might initially look like a project management skills issue (X), but upon exploration it could well be about stakeholder expectation management (Y). Sending Mary on a project management course is very unlikely to sort out her skills in stakeholder management. Exploring what the real driver is, and setting an appropriate objective to address it, enables the desired performance outcome to be achieved in six or twelve months' time, when it comes to evaluating performance.

What is of no use to anyone is for Chris to set a project management improvement objective for Mary when the real issue is that procurement projects are taking longer due to increased complexity and the lack of making business units aware of this. Put another way, setting a project management objective is not going to sort out Mary's lack of effective stakeholder management.

Following this through, Mary could happily focus on developing her project management skills, thinking she's doing great, while Chris is still getting complaints from the business units. Alternatively, Mary could think the objective is insulting to her excellent project-management skills and, as per the Self-Determination Theory of Motivation, which we will cover in later chapters, dismiss the objective from the start, resulting in neither party being happy.

IMPORTANCE OF UNCOVERING PERFORMANCE CONCERN DRIVERS

As we can see from both the questions Chris asked himself about the possible source of Mary's lower-than-expected performance and the dialogue, it's important to uncover the drivers behind a concerning performance before setting the final objective. For Mary, it turned out to be a combination of an unacknowledged increase in project complexity and a lack of stakeholder expectation management causing what I call "noise". It's not really that Mary is a poor performer; it's that a very subtle and unrecognised shift happened that was left to fester. In today's more complex business world, this type of issue is much more prevalent than managers might be aware of.

This is an excellent example of a manager thinking the performance issue is X when it turns out to be Y and why, as managers, it's important to take the time to reflect and do an initial diagnosis of what the performance issue might be.

This insight became evident to me when I managed an operations team. I had a team member, let's call him Zach, who was very good, to the point that when he did actually have an issue with a particular project, he would come into my office and ask for direction. This happened one day and I explained how to go about approaching the issue. It was fixed, but the next day, the same issue arose. I told him what to do again and it was fixed but was again incorrect the following day. A little frustrated that he was continuing to get it wrong several days in a row, I started reflecting on what was going on here. I knew he was excellent at his job; I knew he was quiet, but I also knew he was interested as he was bringing the issue to me. So why wasn't he taking the points I was sharing with him on board?

The following day, the same thing happened, so I decided to change my approach. I explained to him what he needed to do and then I asked him to explain back to me what exactly he was going to do. He started to explain, but then he got to a fork in the road where he could do A or B. So he asked me, "When I get here, do I do A or B?" I answered him, explaining why A was the right choice, and he continued on. He then came to another fork in the road and asked me, "It it C or D?" This continued until he got to the end of the answer. Next day, the work came in perfectly and we never had another issue.

As managers, one of our roles is to develop and coach our team members to be able to do their jobs to the correct standard. Part of that coaching is to figure out what is getting in their way, and often it can be very, very subtle. I could have very easily decided that Zach was good but couldn't figure things out or follow simple instructions. If that had continued, my confirmation bias would have kicked in and I would have sought out evidence to prove my point. In time, I would have started to have a very poor opinion of Zach, which would eventually have become apparent to him, resulting in a decrease in his motivation and performance. Zach and I would have entered into an unnecessary destructive downward spiral. Just to reiterate, Zach was a great performer.

So, getting to the bottom of what is really driving performance concerns is a key part of both management and setting effective objectives. Chris taking the time to figure out that perhaps the performance issue is something subtler than "Mary isn't performing" and bringing that to the meeting to explore with Mary will most likely get a much more positive engagement than telling her she needs to improve her project management skills or she needs to deliver more projects each year.

Following on from Chris and Mary's conversation, they may determine that recognition of the increased complexity and a discussion with the stakeholders is sufficient to sort the issue out so there's no need for a specific objective. Or it could transpire that Mary never really thinks about her stakeholders and that developing her stakeholder management skills is well worth her while, to enhance her future career opportunities. At that point, she will have recognised the benefit to her and is much more likely to engage with and succeed in the objective than if Chris had just told her he was setting this objective for her.

Now, you might argue that, if Mary was any good at stakeholder management, she should have figured out the increased complexity and managed her stakeholders' expectations better and shouldn't need her manager to point this out to her. While there is truth in that, it's worth remembering that Chris struggled with identifying the real issue and he's much more experienced than Mary. It is also part of a manager's role to coach the employee on the subtleties, to assist their development.

Over the next four chapters, we are going to follow Chris, Mary, Jenny, Ray and some more of their colleagues as they explore each of the different objective types, i.e. Role-Specific, Business-Aligned, Technical and Behavioural Development, and how to design effective SMART objectives.

CHAPTER SUMMARY:

As managers, part of our role is to develop the capability and effectiveness of each team member. As part of this process, it is important to recognise the drivers behind the need for an objective. Some objective drivers are very obvious, such as an organisational change or strategic initiative. Other drivers, particularly in relation to objectives being set in response to lower-than-acceptable performance, are more difficult to determine.

In this case, there is a need to take time out and reflect on the possible performance drivers that are resulting in the observable performance. The insights that arise from this reflection can form part of the basis of the performance conversation with this individual, which will contribute to identifying the most appropriate objectives that will really enhance the individual's performance.

Different drivers result in different objective types, which will drive different performance outcomes. Selecting the wrong driver and objective type points an employee in the wrong direction, leading to disappointment, frustration and demotivation and resulting in reduced performance.

Selecting the right driver(s) and objective types points in the direction the employee needs to go to increase their competence, skills and experience and succeed. While it might be difficult, as they learn and practise they see and feel that they are getting different, often better, outcomes. In turn, their confidence grows and their performance increases.

PROMPTS FOR YOU:

Identify someone from your team who would benefit from a behavioural developmental objective and complete the following:

- Describe and note down the observable behaviours of concern.
- Identify five to seven possible reasons that might be contributing to the set of observable behaviours. Try to include two or three possible reasons beyond just the individual, e.g. team dynamics, organisational culture, etc.
- Try to name some possible drivers that might be behind these behaviours.

CHAPTER 5

Exploring Role-Specific SMART Objectives

We're going to focus on exploring role-specific objectives in this chapter. As outlined in Table 2 in the previous chapter, Chris identified the following possible Role-Specific objectives for Mary:

- – SAP procurement project
- – Number of projects per year
- – New to procurement process

Carrying on from the last chapter, we saw SMART Objective 5 outlines how an SAP procurement (X) project could be set out.

SMART Objective 5: SAP Procurement Project

SPECIFIC: Procure SAP implementation consultancy services
MEASURABLE: SAP consultancy services contract in place
ATTAINABLE: Yes, assuming budgetary approval
RELEVANT: Strategic initiative

TimeFrame: *End-month 1:* tender request document approved and distributed
End-month 3: evaluate tender responses
End-month 4: conclude contract with successful candidate

EXPLORING VOLUME-TYPE ROLE-SPECIFIC OBJECTIVE

Upon reflection, Chris determines that it's not the specific project that's the issue, it's the number of projects Mary is completing throughout the year, i.e. the driver is around the volume of projects being completed per year. The question now becomes, "How can Chris set an objective focused on increasing the number of projects to be delivered?"

In effect, this SMART objective is about setting out expectations around how many projects should be delivered per role per year, regardless of who is undertaking the role. It prompts a conversation around project complexity, project size, project duration, etc. and how many projects can be delivered in a year, given other role and organisational commitments. Categorisation of projects might include considering:

- Are all procurement projects of similar size, complexity and duration? If projects are typically two to three months long and of similar complexity in terms of knowledge and skills required, then it's reasonable to expect roughly four or five projects delivered in a 12-month period. This takes annual leave, training, and other aspects of the role's responsibilities expected to be undertaken during the year into account.
- If projects aren't of similar size, complexity, etc. is there a way of categorising them, e.g., vanilla projects (basic, straightforward, short duration, etc.), medium, complex, highly complex. etc. Using an agreed categorisation table, the number and type of projects expected to be delivered during the year could be agreed.
- For example, it could be possible to identify the characteristics that make a project straightforward, as compared to the characteristics that lend increased complexity, such as specific types of tenders or the value of the project or the number of business units that need to input into the tender.

Table 3: Sample Procurement Project Categorisation

PROJECT CATEGORY	DURATION	SIZE/VALUE	COMPLEXITY
VANILLA	1–2 months	<$100,000	Low
MEDIUM	2–4 months	<$500,000	Low—medium
COMPLEX	6–9 months	>$500,000	High
	6–9 months	>$1,000,000	Medium
VERY COMPLEX	9+ months	>$1,000,000	High

Table 3 sets out what a project categorisation grid might look like for a procurement function. In some organisations, these expectations might already be quite clear and explicit within the team, while in other organisations they may be less defined.

If this project categorisation approach is new to Chris and his team, it is something that Chris, as the manager, could invite the team to contribute to during a team meeting or workshop. Building on the principles of change management, the more the team contributes to agreeing the categorisation table, the easier it is for them to accept the expectations that arise from it.

It is also a way to broach the subject with Mary. Maybe she is not aware of the project volume expectations and so isn't thinking in terms of the number of projects she needs to deliver per year. Come objective setting, such an objective won't come as such a surprise to her.

Using Table 3 above, an appropriate objective for Mary might look like:

SMART Objective 6: Annual Project Volumes

SPECIFIC: Deliver three vanilla projects and one complex project as assigned

MEASURABLE: Each assigned project will be delivered within its agreed timeframes, as per project plan, and agreed project outputs as deemed acceptable by the project client

ATTAINABLE: Should be attainable but assumptions and potential constraints and supports should be captured and discussed in each project scope document

RELEVANT: Main purpose of procurement officer role is to run procurement projects

TIMEFRAMES: Each project to be delivered as per timelines agreed during project-planning stage

As we can see, this SMART objective sets out expectations around the number of projects to be delivered in the period. It doesn't specifically name which projects should be delivered, just an indicative number of projects per project category. This removes the need to keep revisiting project-specific objectives based on projects changing, being reassigned, etc. and introduces more flexibility. For example, if projects change throughout the year or have not yet been identified at the time of objective setting, the objective will still be relevant by the end of the year.

Chris could introduce further flexibility by expanding Specific to include:

Specific: Three vanilla projects and one complex project;
or   Three vanilla projects and two medium projects;
or   Three or four vanilla projects and one or two medium projects.

As mentioned previously, if Chris and Mary followed the approach outlined in the SMART Objective 5: SAP Procurement Project example, they would need to set out an objective for every project Mary is expected to work on throughout the year. Some points to consider with using this approach include:

- It is very unlikely that all the procurement needs of the business are known at the beginning of the year.
- It is very likely that procurement needs will change throughout the year.
- If Mary was set four or five project-specific objectives, it would be very difficult to set additional developmental or strategic objectives for Mary as she would likely feel overwhelmed by the sheer number of objectives set.
- For a project-based role, setting individual projects as objectives is the equivalent of listing off the management and cash forecasting tasks for Ray. Mary's job is to manage and deliver procurement projects. Listing off the specific projects for the year isn't stretching or developing her as objectives should do.
- By dealing with the expected volume of projects delivered in a year in one objective, it allows space for other objectives to also be set.

Other examples of role-specific objective type topics include:

- Learning a new system, process or task and taking over responsibility for delivering it, e.g. Ray learning to prepare the cash forecasting outputs for his business units.
- Taking over responsibility for managing a new account, business unit, or client. It may be more complex, technically more difficult, or an increase in volume.
- Increasing the volume of work completed or the consistent standards required.
- Developing and applying a new competence needed to successfully perform the role.

EXPLORING PROCESS-TYPE ROLE-SPECIFIC OBJECTIVE

Let's take a look at an example of a role-specific objective focused on learning a new competency or process. While Mary is experienced and has been in her role for three years, Chris recognises that her colleague, Ron, has only been in the team for a few months and needs some training on the team's procurement process. He initially designs the following objective for Ron:

SMART Objective 7: Learning the Procurement Project Process

SPECIFIC: Learn the procurement project process
MEASURABLE: On-the-job training has been delivered
ATTAINABLE: Yes
RELEVANT: Needed to do the job
TIMEFRAME: End-month 1

Again, it looks specific, it's measurable and time bound, so on the face of it, it looks SMART. However, is this really the objective Chris means to set out? Ron is pretty new to the team so he definitely does need to increase his understanding of the team's processes. It would be very easy for Chris to set this objective for Ron and I've seen countless examples of managers doing this. However, Chris attended the SMART Objective Setting workshop and he now knows better than to set such a limited objective.

This SMART example neatly highlights the issue that we touched on in Chapter 3—I know what *I* mean by this objective; do *you* know what I mean by this objective?

What Chris really means is that Ron will receive the training and he will then apply his new knowledge and skills to increase the quality and timeliness of his tender documents. However, what Ron hears is that once he gets the training, he's achieved his goal. More importantly, that's what this objective documents.

Like Mary and the project management, it would be very easy for Ron to agree to this objective now, achieve it and be delighted to walk into his performance review in six or 12 months' time, knowing that he's knocked this objective out of the ball park.

Chris, on the other hand, has realised that if he set this limited objective, he might get to the review and be very frustrated that Ron still isn't really performing to the right standard and that he's not seeing the expected upswing in Ron's ability to deliver procurement projects. Chris has also realised that he would be forced to agree that, yes, as per the agreed objective, Ron got the on-the-job training and so achieved his objective.

Why does this SMART objective not work for Chris? Chris has recognised that the Measurable agreed is not actually the outcome Chris wants. He doesn't just want the training completed; he wants Ron to take that learning and apply it to the procurement process. In other words, the objective isn't that the training is provided; it's that Ron uses his new knowledge, and related skills, to increase his ability to run projects. Phrasing it like this, we can also see that the Specific outcome isn't particularly well-defined either. A more effectively crafted objective might look something like:

SMART Objective 8: Learning the Procurement Project Process (Revised)

SPECIFIC:	Improve effectiveness of running assigned procurement projects
MEASURABLE:	Projects are approved, first time and on time
ATTAINABLE:	Yes, assuming training and coaching provided
RELEVANT:	Needed to do the job
TIMEFRAME:	*End-month 1:* Training delivered
	End-month 2: Check-in meeting to give feedback and answer questions
	End-month 3: Check-in meeting

End-month 4: Responsible for delivering assigned projects, on an accurate and timely basis

As we can see, by making a few changes, this becomes a very different objective and delivers a very different outcome. With the first objective, the outcome is that Ron increases his understanding of the procurement process, i.e. receipt of training is the output. Is that really what this objective is about? No, it's really about applying the increased knowledge to the tasks and responsibilities of his job.

With the second objective, the outcome is that Ron needs to submit tender documents that are both on time and approved first time. It recognises that as part of developing Ron's ability to achieve this, he needs training; i.e. training is an input needed to achieve the desired output of correctly prepared tender documents.

You might be thinking, *Surely Ron will know he needs to apply the training to his job!* If you're nodding your head, I suggest you consider the assumptions you're making with this thought, as there are likely to be several, but let me share a few points:

- Ron may well appreciate the training and see how it helps him to do his job. However, does this mean he is automatically going to think that having, had this training, he now needs to submit his tender documents on time and with 100% accuracy? From my experience, I'd say that's an extended-elastic-band stretch too far.
- Recalling Carl Jung's theory of how people receive new information, Ron may have a preference for Sensing and so is more likely to focus on what has been articulated in the objective rather than what might be implied or expected by Chris.
- There's a concept called "knowledge assimilation" that I rarely hear mentioned in business literature but is extremely important for both an individual's and the business' performance. It's such a driver of performance that every company I have ever worked with on behavioural competencies has identified it as a key differentiator of performance while not knowing what it is called. Knowledge assimilation is the ability to absorb new knowledge and learn new skills and apply them in different situations. I can assure you that not every employee demonstrates this ability while most managers do demonstrate it.

So, applying your own standards and assuming, "Of course Ron will know to apply the knowledge," is not automatically true.

- Part of the beauty of using SMART effectively is that it generates a two-way conversation, closing the gap between assumptions on both sides. If Chris sets the first objective and walks out thinking, *That's grand, I'll start seeing better quality work coming from Ron soon,* while Ron walks out thinking, *It'll be good to get a bit of training,* Chris is likely to get irritated as his expectations aren't met. Ron is going to be oblivious as to why he's the source of Chris' irritation, but he's likely to feel the impact of it. Low-level tension and conflict are going to soon follow, resulting in energy being diverted away from the work, towards managing the emotions.

Setting the first objective sets up a huge potential for conflict six or 12 months down the line before Chris and Ron have even finished the meeting. This may seem obvious when pointed out, but given our fast-paced work environment and human tendencies to assume other people's perceptions are the same as ours, this is a very common occurrence across all industries.

In comparison, setting the second objective clearly states the expected outcome of the training, i.e. that the quality of work will improve. It indicates the support that will be provided via the initial on-the-job training and the monthly check-in meetings. Indicating that feedback will be given puts Ron on notice that he should expect feedback, so it shouldn't come as a surprise to him when feedback is given. The map outlined under Timeframe gives Ron a sense of the timings and expectations of when he should be able to successfully prepare tender documents. Ron should leave this objective-setting meeting with a clear understanding that, as of the end of month four, he is responsible for producing high-quality tender documents. This isn't a last-minute.com objective that he can successfully achieve in the last month of the performance period.

MANAGER-LEVEL ROLE-SPECIFIC OBJECTIVE EXAMPLE

The two objectives we have just looked at for Mary and Ray, while role-specific, could be considered as quite technical. What if we manage a team of managers who manage their own teams and we'd like to set a role-specific objective for a manager?

One of my all-time-favourite objectives I ever worked through was with an executive team in an international tech company. These were ex-Gillette, ex-P&G, all very seasoned executives. I asked for an example of an objective they wanted to work through, so a voice piped up with setting an objective for managers, around staff retention. I'll describe the mood in the room as *"Let's see you make a SMART objective out of that!"*

Taking a deep breath, wondering how I was going to make sense of this one, I noted down the general topic under "Specific" and the conversation went something like this:

Me: How will we measure this?
Ans: 100% retention.

Me: Do we want 100% retention?
Ans: Yes.

Me: Do we?
Ans: Yes, well… Maybe not.

Me: What type of retention do we want?
Ans: We want to keep the top performers … and the good performers … and the decent performers.

Me: So, what level of retention do we want?
Ans: About 95% retention.

Me: And is the retention all the same?
Ans: Huh?

Me: Do we want to keep the same level of retention of the top performers as the decent performers?
Ans: Well, we'd like to keep all of the top performers and we'd be happy to keep most of the good and decent performers. We're quite happy for the poor performers to leave.

Me: Okay, so what would the measurement look like?

Ans: 100% of top performers, 90% of good performers.

Me: So, how will we know who's who?

Ans: Well, we'd need to identify and agree who falls into which category.

Me: Okay, so we'd need to categorise the employees into three groups—A: Top Performers, B: Good Performers, C: Average.

Ans: Yes, that makes sense.

Me: Okay, so we know the measurement. Is this attainable?

Ans: Yes.

Me: Is it? (You get the drift here; for all their seniority and experience, very little thought had been given over to this type of stuff before this workshop).

Ans: Well…

Me: What if someone leaves because they're moving to Australia with their other half? Is the manager going to be held responsible for that?

Ans: Well, no.

Me: Or if they decide to change career and go back to college?

Ans: Eh, no.

Me: Right, so what are the managers going to be held responsible for?

Ans: Well, they could be held responsible for retaining staff that are staying within a country we work in and staying within the industry; so holding on to people who are leaving for work-related reasons rather than for personal reasons.

Me: Right, and to what degree?

Ans: What?

Me: Well, how far do you expect managers to go to retain someone who's a high performer in their own role but leaves a trail of destruction in their wake? Or a good employee who is going around telling their colleagues that they were going to leave but now they're staying for an extra five grand?

Ans: Well…

As you can see, some objectives come with constraints that might well be outside the employee's control. The last thing you want to have to do with a good manager is have to tell them they have failed in their retention objective because a poor performer from their team has left, even though you'd throw a party to celebrate their departure, or that they failed because a good employee left due to their granny dying, prompting them to leave for a trek around India to find themselves. I'll leave your imagination to conjure up the sense of injustice and resentment that would likely follow.

We ended up with an objective that looked something like this:

SMART Objective 9: Active Retention of Talent

SPECIFIC: Actively retain talent

MEASURABLE: Retain 95% of top talent, 90% of good talent staying within industry/function, on an annual basis

ATTAINABLE: If properly managed, led, developed and engaged, should be within remit to retain people staying within the industry/ function

RELEVANT: Costly to hire and bed-in new employees. Slows down function's ability to deliver outputs

TIMEFRAMES: *End-month 1:* Agree the Top Talent, Good Talent and Talent lists
End-month 2: Sign off on engagement strategy plans to engage appropriately with each group
End-month 3 onwards: Implement strategies, as per plans
Quarterly: Check-in meeting to review retention and engagement levels and wider organisational issues that might be negatively impacting retention

As you can see, by the end we had created a pretty solid objective. So, I couldn't resist asking them:

Me: Would you be happy to set this objective with your senior managers?

Ans: Yes.

Me: At the start, did you think we'd get such a solid objective?

Ans: No.

LEARNING POINTS FROM THIS SMART OBJECTIVE

SPECIFIC

Setting the objective up, as outlined above, does a few things. For managers that are set this objective, it clearly indicates an expectation of responsibility for employee retention. A high staff turnover isn't something they can just excuse away or blame on others. I've witnessed numerous conversations where the list of excuses and reasons for why Johnny, Clare and Paul left is endless. In these conversations, all I see is the pattern of staff turnover.

MEASUREMENT

Since we have defined the measure as to whether departed staff have stayed in the industry and/or function, either they did or they didn't. This measure makes it a lot more black and white to evaluate and removes the need to listen to all the reasons why.

TIMEFRAME

The way the Timeframe roadmap is set out indicates that this is an ongoing objective. This is important to highlight because this is not the type of objective that once completed for this performance cycle is done and dusted. It's a role-specific objective that:

a. Ensures the manager has set out a talent retention strategy
b. Sets out a timeframe as to when the manager is going to have the infrastructure of talent retention (i.e. the lists, the strategy plans for each group, etc.) in place

    c.   Indicates the senior manager's responsibility in retaining talent on an ongoing basis

So, success for the manager will be twofold: (1) to get the process designed and up and running; and (2) ongoing delivery for the next X number of years they're in the role.

OBJECTIVE PURPOSE

What the above objective is really getting at is the manager's responsibility to manage their team's retention, either directly and indirectly, depending on their level of management. For example, if the manager is directly managing a team of employees, then they are directly responsible for ensuring the retention of talent and that they have the ability to engage with team members in a way that they can monitor engagement levels and surface problems before they become an issue.

If the manager manages a team of managers, i.e. a senior manager, they are directly responsible for retaining their own direct reports, i.e. the managers, while indirectly responsible for ensuring each of their managers is actively retaining their talent. So, the senior manager's strategy might include working with managers to ensure they are properly managing their team members and coaching them through how to deal with issues. In a nutshell, it's an objective around ensuring managers at all levels are both (a) managing their people and (b) managing them effectively.

OBJECTIVE DRIVERS

Taking the time to understand the drivers as to why talent isn't already been actively managed should shed some light as to why the objective is needed and what it needs to cover. One typical driver that might prompt such an objective is the level of staff turnover. It could be across the whole organisation and there is a strategic focus across the organisation to reduce it. Or it could be that this particular team or function has high employee turnover or faces a very tight labour market for their specific skills so they want to retain as many people as possible.

As set out above, this is a Role-Specific objective, based on an assumption that there is no formal retention strategy or process infrastructure. If a formal retention strategy and process exists within in the organisation, the objective can be adjusted accordingly, to reflect this. This objective, as set out, also assumes that the manager knows how to identify retention strategies and has the necessary skills to execute them. In the event that the manager or senior manager doesn't know how to approach this, the objective can be expanded to become a Role-Specific objective with a Developmental aspect to it.

CHAPTER SUMMARY:

Role-Specific objectives are objectives that provide direction to an employee, so that they are performing the role in accordance with the needs of the team, function, and organisation as a whole. They call out specific aspects of a role that a job description cannot do. They may be driven by organisational initiatives, e.g. the talent retention example, or they may be specific to the individual, e.g. taking over responsibility for a particular process or account.

When preparing for objective setting, it is important to identify the drivers to ensure that a role-specific objective is the correct objective type to set.

When constructing Role-Specific objectives, clearly articulate the desired outcome you're looking for and ensure that the objective is structured in such a way that it delivers that outcome, rather than some output required to achieve the outcome. Role-specific objectives may also include aspects of developmental objectives.

PROMPTS FOR YOU:

Note down the volume outputs expected for each of the roles within your team. If there are categories of complexity, note down the categorisation criteria.

Share and/or explore the categories and criteria with your team, if not already done.

Consider someone from your team whom you want to set a role-specific objective for. What are the drivers behind the need for this objective?

CHAPTER 6

Exploring Business-Aligned SMART Objectives

In order to deliver business strategies, many employees are assigned objectives that link to the business objectives or strategy. In this chapter, we'll explore how best to set this objective type in detail. As explained in the Introduction, there is a whole process behind the cascading of strategy down to functional, team and individual objectives, which is beyond the scope of this book. For this book's purpose, we'll define a business-aligned objective as any objective that aligns with and is part of the delivery of the business strategy, whether it be the corporate strategy, the business strategy, business plan or functional strategy.

As we saw with Ray, he was charged with implementing SAP in his team and this objective directly supports the company's strategic objective of getting better insight into the running of the business via the decision to install and implement SAP.

In reality, business-related objectives are more likely to be assigned to more experienced and/or more senior employees, particularly at different levels of management, as more junior employees are likely to be busy with the work associated with the business-as-usual processes and outputs of their function. Junior or inexperienced employees are more likely to be assigned business-aligned objectives as the implementation stage approaches.

For example, in Chris's team, Rose and Ken, the administrators, are likely to be busy with ensuring all tender queries are responded to and the tender calendar is kept up to date. Paula, the contracts manager, on the other hand, might be tasked with objectives that have a more obvious line of sight to the company's strategy, such as ensuring the SAP supplier contract scope is aligned to meet the company's needs.

I point this out because not everyone in an organisation will always see a direct link between their objectives and the strategy in every performance period. For example, Rose and Ken might not be directly impacted by the SAP company strategy objective until SAP is being implemented, which could be one or two performance cycles down the line. However, they should be able to see that by ensuring tenders are in place and relevant products and services are continuously available to business units, their role is directly contributing to the company achieving its purpose.

Chris and Jenny both report into Rob, the finance director. Rob, and his colleague Ryan, the IT director, have been charged with implementing SAP. They're going to need input across all the functions while jointly being held responsible for SAP's timely and successful implementation. Rob and Ryan met and agreed that Finance's role is to map out the financial processes across the organisation that need to be incorporated into SAP, while IT's role is to define the company's IT requirements and manage the installation and data transfer. They have joint responsibility to identify the best consulting services provider to meet company's overall needs. They also identified that HR needs to play a role in arranging the training while all functions need to engage with the implementation and incorporation of the new system into functional processes. However, Rob and Ryan are being held jointly responsible for delivering the business objective.

Depending on the size and complexity of the company, this could be a six-month, 12-month or even 24-month project and is likely to extend beyond one performance cycle. So it's important that Rob and Ryan agree the timescale for the stages of this project and flag it to the rest of the executive team so they are aware of their responsibilities in this business objective and the implications for their teams.

As Rob sees it, Finance's involvement in this business objective is twofold: (1) to scope out the finance function's SAP requirements; and (2) to procure the SAP consulting services that will be required to assist with the transition. Once the consultants are in place, he figures there'll be ongoing contract management, which falls into BAU (business-as-usual), and input into designing the finance processes on SAP, which he identifies as a business-aligned project. Once that's done, there will be a functional project to migrate to and implement SAP throughout the function. Finally, there will be the sorting out of teething problems.

Rob also recognises that he will need someone in the team to manage the project on behalf of the finance function from start to finish. This person will work closely with the project manager but will be Rob's eyes and ears, representing Finance and ensuring the finance function is executing its assigned tasks on a timely and accurate basis. This is expected to be a 24-month project so Rob has mapped the objectives out as follows:

Table 4: Finance Team's SAP Project Timeline & Objectives

STAGE & TIMEFRAME	OBJECTIVES	ASSIGNED TO	OBJECTIVE TYPE
PROJECT COORDINATOR MONTHS 1–24	Manages Finance's project deliverables, monitors progress & manages issues	Senior person in finance function	Business-aligned project
PROJECT SCOPING MONTHS 1–6	Finance function's SAP requirements	All finance teams	Business-aligned project
	SAP consultant procurement requirements	Procurement	Business-aligned project
	Tender process	Procurement	BAU—Role specific
CONTRACT MANAGEMENT MONTH 5—FINAL INVOICE PAID	Invoice management	Accounts payable	BAU—Role specific
	Contract account management	Procurement	BAU—Role specific
FINANCE PROCESS MAPPING MONTHS 6–9	Map all finance function processes	All Finance teams	Business-aligned project

SAP DATA TRANSFER MONTHS 9–18	Ensure data transfer & finance processes on SAP work	All Finance teams	Business-aligned project
TRAINING MONTHS 15–18	Learn how to use SAP for relevant finance processes	All Finance staff	What Competence
PARALLEL PROCESSING MONTHS 18–21	Process data on both systems & resolve differences	All Finance staff	Business-aligned project
SAP ONLY PROCESSING MONTHS 22–24	100% processing & reporting via SAP; issue resolution	All Finance staff	BAU—Role specific

Looking at Rob's table, we can see the following:

- While, on the whole, this is a business strategy objective, some aspects fall into BAU for some teams, e.g. the tender process is a specific procurement project in a BAU process.
- Some teams will be charged with specific aspects of the project, e.g. procurement and accounts payable.
- Some aspects will require input from all the teams within the function, e.g. the project scoping and process mapping. However, not everyone from each team will be involved. It is likely that one or two people from each team will be assigned, requiring a relevant objective. It is also likely that they will be chosen from the more experienced employees.
- Some aspects require all finance staff to participate, e.g. learning the SAP system and changes to the finance processes and reporting, and they will require a relevant objective.
- If the performance cycle is annual, we can see that some people within Finance, e.g. staff members preparing financial statements, won't see an objective in relation to this strategic objective until year two while others will be involved in both years one and two.

- The organisation's approach to PM is implied in Rob's table, i.e. if the organisation uses Agile, then the process mapping will be captured following the Agile methodology.

Rob decides he'll design a year one business-aligned objective and assign it to each of his direct reports. He will leave them to assign the related work accordingly. He sets the following objective:

SMART Objective 10: SAP Implementation Year 1

SPECIFIC:	Successfully manage team's appropriate contribution to assigned elements of SAP design and implementation project plan
MEASURABLE:	No avoidable project issues arise due to team's input to mapped processes and data transferred. Team's contribution, cooperation and solution focus is consistently observed and no complaints escalated
ATTAINABLE:	Should be, assuming project proceeds; issues and concerns to be raised on timely basis
RELEVANT:	Successful SAP implementation allows for more timely business decision-making
TIMEFRAME:	*End-month 1:* ID & assign suitable person/people to represent team on project *Months 2–6:* Ensure appropriate team participation, as project plan requires *Months 6–12:* Ensure team's processes are accurately mapped and required data transfer is signed off and accurate

LEARNING POINTS FROM THIS SMART OBJECTIVE

SPECIFIC

Looking at the above objective, Rob is clearly indicating that his managers are responsible for ensuring this project is supported by their team but is not suggesting that the managers undertake the project. This is captured in how the Specific is phrased—manage team's contribution to project, as assigned.

He has left it sufficiently loose to allow for project-planning changes but is still holding the manager responsible to ensure their team's contribution is delivered.

MEASUREMENT

It would be very easy for Rob to just measure this objective's success as "processes are mapped and data transferred into SAP". He could definitely stand over these criteria as tangible, hard metrics that can be easily measured. However, Rob's measurement criteria for successful delivery of this project go beyond measuring success by using just the hard metrics. He has incorporated the quality standard he expects of the process mapping and data transfer.

Rob proposes to measure quality by "no avoidable project issues arise..." He is implying here that no issues should arise that, down the line, were identified as due to the team's poor input or, indeed, lack of input, i.e. he is going to measure the success of this project by how thoroughly the team helped the project succeed and by the number of avoidable issues that arise later on, due to the team not sharing or identifying issues at the appropriate time. By including this, Rob is sending out a clear message that going through the motions won't do.

What's an "avoidable" issue? Most likely, it will be defined during the project as "why didn't you share this at the beginning?" but it's fair to say that, collectively, there will be a recognition that X could have been avoided if we had known about it earlier on. Phrasing the objective this way ensures the manager, while not doing the detailed work of the project, recognises that they are very much being held responsible for the team's contribution to and engagement with the project.

Avoidable issues aren't the only thing Rob is going to measure the success of this objective on. As it turns out, he has been involved in several large-scale technology changes and knows exactly how the interpersonal interplays impact on delivery success. He has experienced situations where, "Yes, we eventually got accurately mapped processes etc., but we also got conflict, subtle sabotage, resentment and projects taking three times as long as they should have." So Rob has also included a softer metric in the form of cooperation, level of contribution (this could also be termed "engagement") and being solution focused.

He is seeking to ensure that each of his teams "shows up" to this project. He doesn't want to hear complaints that the accounts payable team keep cancelling their workshops or that Chris's procurement team turn up but keep constantly pointing out what could go wrong. He recognises that projects can overrun for all sorts of reasons outside of the project team's control, but he also knows that a subtle withdrawal of cooperation is often a key factor in slowing projects down. So, he is measuring the success of this project not just on the basis of achieving the outputs, i.e. mapped processes and data transfer, but also on the sense of engagement of the finance team's contribution to and support of the project. In effect, he is holding his managers accountable for ensuring there is no blowback on the finance function.

ATTAINABLE

Again, Rob has seen numerous organisational projects launched and he's quite aware that issues may arise in other parts of the project team. Under "Attainable", he recognises that other teams could adversely impact the project. For example, IT could assign a poor or inexperienced project manager (PM) to this project or the project board continuously fail to make decisions. Either of these scenarios would negatively impact the project's success.

By including "issues and concerns to be raised on a timely basis" under "Attainable" Rob is doing two things. Firstly, he is recognising that some constraints are out of the managers' sphere of control while indicating the support he is willing to provide to his managers, i.e. that they can raise issues around their concerns on the running of the project.

Secondly, he is also indicating to them that they need to do so on a timely basis. He doesn't want to be sitting across from a manager in 12 months' time evaluating the project as having been a failure only for the manager to give him a litany of excuses about the quality of the communication or the lack of decision-making, or any of the other million excuses that could be offered up, and for this to be the first time he's hearing about them.

Rob is clearly indicating that any issues from other quarters need to be escalated on a timely basis so that they can be sorted out and he's not going to accept excuses after the fact. While recognising things go wrong, he is holding his managers responsible for taking ownership for escalating issues outside of their control, to ensure they get them resolved on a timely basis.

TIMEFRAME

Finally, on the timeframes, Rob could have said something along the lines of "timeframes and deadlines as per project plan" and this might well have been appropriate and sufficient.

One point of note, though, is in relation to the assigning of a suitable person. By indicating a timeframe on this, Rob demonstrates that, even if the project doesn't start for a month or two, his managers have pulled together the finance function's project team. It could be that he wants to review the list of proposed people and arrange to meet them. He might want to have a project kick-off meeting, where he can set out his expectations of their contribution to the project, provide direction on what to do if they run into difficulties, etc. By including this step, Rob is indicating that he expects his managers to intentionally think about and assign a suitable person, rather than it be a last-minute and thoughtless decision.

Rob's objective might seem like too much planning or thinking, but stepping back and seeing the wider picture, this is a strategic objective for the business and most likely a huge investment. There will be high expectations and a high level of interest from the CEO, the board and the executive team. Taking the time to properly map out and frame the objective and measurement of its success is an important task of management.

YEAR ONE INVOLVEMENT

In year one of this project, only a handful of people within Finance will be involved with it, i.e. one, or maybe two, representative(s) from each team, their team managers, the finance function's project coordinator and Rob. One level, i.e. the team representatives, will be doing most of the work while the team managers will be reviewing and monitoring the work, providing guidance and reporting. The project coordinator will be monitoring the overall project, from the finance function's perspective, anticipating potential issues and ensuring each team is in a position to meet their relevant deadlines. This may be Rob or he may assign it to an experienced senior manager. Rob will be taking an overall interest in the project and working with Ryan and other functional heads to sort out escalated issues.

Rob has created a business-aligned objective designed to be used with all of his mangers as each manager's team will need to participate in this strategic objective. To summarise the objective, it is to ensure that each team contributes to and engages appropriately with the project so that it succeeds company-wide. However, it is not the only objective that will be set in relation to this initiative. Rob expects his managers to break it down further and assign appropriate objectives within their own teams.

For example, Rob specifies his managers' objective as:

> *Successfully manage team's appropriate contribution to assigned elements of SAP design & implementation project plan.*

In turn, Jenny has assigned Ray to be her team's representative on this project, so she might define his specific objective as:

> *Successfully represents financial management team's SAP needs and actively contributes to and delivers all assigned project tasks.*

We can see that, while these objectives are related to the overall company objective and strategic initiative, they are tailored to different levels of responsibility and contribution. In performance-management terms, Jenny's objective from Rob has been cascaded down to Ray. Jenny is still responsible for ensuring her team contributes effectively, but she has assigned the day-to-day work to Ray.

YEAR TWO INVOLVEMENT

In year two of this project, everyone within the function will be involved, by attending training, parallel processing, testing and moving over to SAP, so it would be reasonable to expect that, in year two, everybody within the function will be assigned some sort of objective aligned with this strategic goal.

CHAPTER SUMMARY:

A business-aligned objective is one aligned to the organisation's strategy. It is likely to be assigned to more experienced and/or senior employees and managers. Depending on the size of the strategic initiative, several objectives may be developed, targeted to different levels of contribution and responsibility.

In the case of business-aligned objectives, the driver is coming directly from the company's strategy or business plan, so when designing this type of objective, identifying the driver becomes less important. On the other hand, clarifying the stages and expected timeframes of the strategic initiatives, the level of involvement and input required, the desired outcomes and how they might be measured are important inputs into effectively designing this type of objective.

While the key driver of a business-aligned objective is the strategy, depending on the individual there could also be a developmental aspect to it as well. In such circumstances, clearly identifying and articulating the developmental drivers will inform the developmental aspects of the objective.

PROMPTS FOR YOU:

Identify an imminent business-aligned initiative that your team is expected to be involved in. If there are no business-aligned initiatives, consider functional or team initiatives that you would like the team to become involved in.

Consider the different levels of involvement needed and identify who on the team is best positioned to provide each level.

For one team member, consider whether there is also a developmental aspect for them. If so, identify whether it is a technical or behavioural need and what the driver(s) behind that developmental need is.

CHAPTER 7

Exploring Technical Developmental SMART Objectives

As we saw in Chapter 1, developmental objectives are those objectives aimed at developing the employee's competencies, be they technical or behavioural. They may overlap with or be linked to aspects of other objective types. For example, Jenny and Ray might decide that Ray needs to obtain a project management (PM) qualification as part of his SAP objective. This PM qualification might be set out as a separate developmental objective but linked to the SAP objective or incorporated into the SAP objective, depending on how Jenny and Ray set it out.

In this chapter, we'll explore technical developmental objectives, while in Chapter 8 we'll take a look at behavioural objectives.

Here's an example of how many managers typically set out a developmental objective:

SMART Objective 11: Developing Project Management Skills

SPECIFIC: Develop PM skills
MEASURABLE: Get the PM certificate
ATTAINABLE: Yes, courses run regularly
RELEVANT: Improve PM skills

TIMEFRAME: End-month 3

Take a minute and consider what outcome you think this objective will result in.

Exactly, it will result in Ray getting a certificate in PM, which Ray will be delighted to produce during the review as proof of achieving this goal. The question for Jenny is: was that the outcome she wanted or expected? It's highly unlikely that Ray getting his certificate was Jenny's ideal outcome from this objective. It is much more likely that, while she's delighted that Ray got the certificate, she now wants him to put that newfound knowledge to work in better managing and contributing to projects.

Since "attending a course" or "getting a certificate" is a very tangible measurement, it's very easy to agree that something along these lines is the measurement of success in achieving a developmental objective. However, Jenny attended the SMART workshop and recognises that this isn't the outcome she wants Ray to achieve. She wants him to effectively start running projects and recognises that he needs the knowledge to understand the company's project management methodology as part of being successful. So, Jenny and Ray craft the following objective:

SMART Objective 12: Developing Project Management Skills Revised

SPECIFIC: Successfully manage the financial management team's assigned SAP tasks and ensure all inputs and outputs are delivered accurately and timely

MEASURABLE: PM certificate obtained; all relevant project deadlines are met; no justified complaints or negative feedback

ATTAINABLE: Yes, assuming project proceeds and attending PM course is approved

RELEVANT: Supports the delivery of a strategic initiative

TIMEFRAME: *End-month 1:* Source and sign up for PM certification; attend all project meetings; prepare team's project plan; gain approval of project plan, communicate plan and team member task assignment proposal

End-month 2: Obtain PM certification and incorporate learning into own project delivery

Months 2–12: Manage team's project plan, as per schedule

Chair finance management team's monthly project update meeting

Ensure team meets all SAP project plan requirements each month

As we can see, this objective combines the technical development objective of "increasing competence in project management" with the business-aligned objective of "representing the financial management team on SAP project". In effect, Jenny is saying that she wants Ray to improve his understanding of and ability to run projects by attending the PM course and applying the knowledge and understanding to the SAP project.

LEARNING POINTS FROM THIS SMART OBJECTIVE

Working through the revised objective, the need for the PM training and certification is one element in the roadmap outlined under Timeframe. It acknowledges that it needs to be achieved but only as a step along the way of managing the project for the team. Jenny wants Ray to take responsibility to deliver this project rather than just get the PM qualification.

As we saw earlier, focusing on the training as the measurable outcome of the objective is a very common and understandable mistake managers make when using SMART. It is something that can be measured and often seems more tangible that the purpose of the training, which is to take over the responsibility of doing something. When setting a Developmental Objective, it's important to keep asking the question—what is the desired outcome of this objective?

MEASURABLE

Under Measurable, like Rob, Jenny has linked feedback from others to Ray's success. So it's not enough for Ray to deliver the project; he has also driven the SAP project manager round the bend. However, she also recognises the frailty of humans and will discount spurious complaints. This should allay any concerns Ray may have over unjustified or unfair complaints.

While the opportunity for conflict to arise, due to a fair complaint, is still there, it certainly puts Ray on notice that the possibility of complaints being linked to the evaluation of his performance exists.

ATTAINABLE

Under Attainable, Jenny has also indicated possible constraints, in this case that the cost of the course is approved. Another obvious constraint might be if a suitable course can be sourced within the timeframe. There are many different types of possible constraints and something that might be a possible constraint in one organisation, e.g. course approval, might not be an issue in another.

TIMEFRAME

Under Timeframe, we can see that Jenny and Ray have agreed an indicative roadmap. The first couple of months explicitly call out the need for the development of Ray's technical competence in project management while also getting to grips with the overall SAP project and the team's required contributions. The rest of the period indicates a monthly cycle of execution, monitoring and updates.

As you read this, you might be thinking, *Well, I'd phrase it like this,* or, *I'd include that,* etc. There are many ways such an objective could be written and be effective in shaping the desired outcome. The specifics of the situation need to be taken into consideration, which will naturally lead to tweaks and changes. As long as they contribute to and support the outcome you, as the manager, are looking for, those variations are all valid too. The purpose here is to get managers recognising and thinking about the different aspects and identifying available options to approach them.

SUPPORT TYPES FOR DEVELOPMENTAL OBJECTIVE SUCCESS

In relation to support, what support does this objective call out?

TRAINING SUPPORT

We already noted above that this objective requires the organisation's support to pay for and allow the time for Ray to attend and obtain the PM certificate.

Something for Jenny to consider is if there are any constraints at the organisational level that will prevent the agreed training support being provided. For example, has the company cracked down on external courses? Or has the training budget for the year been used up? Are there alternative ways to access the skills and knowledge required?

TEAM SUPPORT

As we saw in Chapter 2, Jenny intends to assign Anna and Carol, the other team members, objectives that will support the overall delivery of this objective. They need to support the project by accepting and delivering the tasks they are assigned as part of their objectives. At the end of month one, as part of supporting project buy-in, the team's project plan needs to be approved. Implicitly, Jenny needs to sign off on this, which likely would have been discussed at the objective-setting meeting. However, if the team is included in this sign-off process, it increases their support of the objective.

In addition, it also requires support through the monthly team meeting that Jenny and other team members will need to regularly attend. Most likely, this won't be a problem for Jenny as she will want to keep an eye on this objective because it feeds into her objective. Carol and Anna are also likely to want to attend as their objectives are tied into this project.

However, if there are already five monthly meetings scheduled, will this additional monthly meeting *really* happen? Has the team got 20 other projects on their collective plate along with all the weekly cash forecasting and monthly management accounts? Will Carol and Anna really find the time to support this objective along with their other projects?

NAVIGATING CULTURAL DYNAMICS SUPPORT

The training example is a straightforward, clear-cut example of support. Less clear is how to deal with and provide support to navigating the cultural dynamics that torpedo many a good objective. For example, setting an objective that requires cooperation from another function or another person, when even the dogs on the street know they're very unlikely to cooperate, is probably not going to succeed. While the nitty gritty of specific cultural dynamics don't need to be discussed, an acknowledgement of the possibility that they could arise and some guidance as to how to deal with them, if they do arise, would be sufficient at the objective-setting stage.

If the manager doesn't invite a proper two-way conversation about those concerns, the employee may well agree to the objective at the meeting but not buy into it. Let's be clear here; an employee agreeing to an objective that they are pretty sure isn't going to succeed, for reasons outside of their control or influence, and isn't invited to express those concerns is not buying into the objective. They've acquiesced to it. As we will see when we explore Self-Determination Theory in Chapter 9, it's highly unlikely that the employee is going to put much effort into an objective they figure is already doomed. A small bit of reflection, by the manager, at the planning stage would highlight this.

MANAGEMENT SUPPORT

Jenny needs to identify what level of management support she needs to give Ray and what she needs in return. One clear area is what is expected in relation to progress and communication. For example, Jenny may be comfortable with Ray running with the project and is happy for him to keep her in the loop through monthly summary updates. Or she might only want to hear about things going wrong or off-track.

Another area Ray is likely to need guidance on is decision-making, e.g. who is responsible for making what decisions. Which ones are within his remit, which ones need to be brought to Jenny and which ones need to escalated to Rob, Ryan or the executive team?

Jenny also needs to determine what level of support Ray needs from her, as his manager, which we will cover under Coaching Support.

On a broader note on management support, as manager, what level of support are you really in a position to provide? It's not just *this* employee with *this* objective who needs support. It's providing support within the context of all the support required for all the other objectives for this person, and the rest of the team, alongside your own commitments and BAU work. I've seen managers agree to a level of support that I can just tell they're not going to be in a position to provide. While their intentions come from a good place, a promise not fulfilled leads to trust issues, which damages the relationship. Clearly acknowledging that you will be busy but you give them full permission to hound you or put a meeting in their diary goes a long way to (re-)assuring the employee that it's okay to push for the agreed support or that they know what they have permission to do if they're not getting it.

COACHING AND MENTORING SUPPORT

A huge side benefit for both Jenny and Ray meeting to agree the project plan, a month into the objective, is that it gives Ray the chance to discuss concerns such as correct level of detail or how to gain agreement on resources prior to the project plan being shared with others. He also gets to hear how Jenny likes projects to be run within her team, what the expectations of the wider organisation are, what templates to use, the organisational dos and don'ts, etc.

Since this is an objective driven by the need to build Ray's project management (PM) competence, it's important that both he and Jenny get a chance to discuss performance expectations as the competence is being built. It's a bit like learning to drive a car. There's no point being left to your own devices to learn how to drive, pick up a load of bad habits and then spend a fortune trying to iron them all away. These interactions are key to building up Ray's confidence and Jenny's trust in his ability to run future projects. Having these types of coaching meetings is also part of the role of manager.

For managers reading this who might be thinking, *I wouldn't have the time to sit with Ray and have all those check-in meetings with him,* think about who in the team would be available to sit with him and whose judgement, skills and knowledge on the subject you trust to steer him in a way acceptable to you. It might be a management-development-type objective that could be agreed with them as part of their own career development, resulting in a win-win-win for them, you as manager, and your own "Ray".

Another route Jenny could explore is identifying someone within the organisation who could mentor Ray. In Ray's case, it could be a seasoned PM, who could guide him and provide advice on how to deal with tricky situations, particularly how to deal with the cultural dynamics. They could meet regularly throughout the project, providing ongoing support tailored to the issues that arise.

SUPPORT SUMMARY

Understanding the different types of support and options to provide it throughout the relevant timeframe hugely influences the likely outcome of any objective. I've seen so many managers set out objectives and not think about any of this stuff. As we tease through an objective or two, it transpires that the manager inevitably is making huge assumptions that they haven't recognised or articulated. Some of those assumptions are of the "make or break" type.

If, for example, your company has frozen all external training and you've agreed that an employee goes on an external course as part of their objective, this objective is doomed before you've even left the room. A little bit of thought would logically tell us this and yet managers still go ahead and agree to such an objective without thinking.

To summarise, developmental objectives, be they technical or behavioural, often require some level of support. As we have seen, there are a range of different support types and any given developmental objective may pull aspects from different support types, as shown in Table 5: Support Types & Examples:

Table 5: Support Types & Examples

Support Type	Examples
Training & Learning	On-the-job, internal or external training courses; certificates & accreditations; higher education courses; books & research
Team	Providing feedback & input; attending & contributing to related meetings; mentoring; adjusting behavioural patterns
Navigating Cultural Dynamics	Insights & mentoring on how to recognise and/or deal with certain cultural dynamics; giving direction on how to deal with situations or navigate the culture
Management	Making timely decisions; providing face time to discuss issues; giving permission; resources
Coaching & Mentoring	Manager-as-coach; assign internal or external coach or mentor

CHAPTER SUMMARY

Technical developmental objectives focus on building the technical capability of the employee so that they can successfully deliver the outputs and/or outcomes of their role or support business-aligned objectives. They may iterate expectations around quality, standards, deadlines, and volume, but they typically do include some sort of training, coaching, feedback, and support that will help them take over or improve their ability to complete aspects of their role or deliver strategic outputs or outcomes.

Technical developmental objectives are likely to support Role-Specific or Business-Aligned objectives rather than objectives that sit on their own. However, this type of objective could be set in one performance cycle in anticipation of applying the increased technical competence in the following performance cycle. For example, Jenny and Ray could have identified Ray's interest in developing his ability to run projects in one performance cycle so that when a suitable project arose, he could be assigned to running it in some later performance cycle.

PROMPTS FOR YOU:

For each of the support types, identify the usual ways these supports are currently provided within your team, function and/or organisation. Identify two or three additional ways support could be provided for each support team.

CHAPTER 8

Exploring Behavioural Developmental SMART Objectives

As we saw in Chapter 1, the other type of developmental objective focuses on developing behavioural competencies. This type of objective focuses on developing the "*how*" a person approaches their role and it covers out a lot of what we would typically consider the "soft" skills of work. For more junior levels, it would include skills such as communication, problem solving, analysis, influencing up, participating effectively in meetings, team cooperation, interpersonal skills, etc.

For managers or more senior individual contributors, it could include skills such as 360 influencing, communicating and story-telling, building trust, chairing meetings, judgement, anticipation, motivating others, building a network, stakeholder management, etc.

Whatever it is about setting technical, metric-driven objectives, in my experience managers don't even know where to start with setting this type of objective. They struggle with articulating what the real issue is, diagnosing what needs to change, and identifying a plan to close the competency gap. Let's take a look at a few examples to help us understand behavioural developmental objectives a bit better.

BEHAVIOURAL EXAMPLE 1: STAKEHOLDER MANAGEMENT

Rob's colleague and head of IT, Ryan, has a team of 20, many of them highly competent in running projects. The SAP project is a high-profile project so he's putting in his best project manager (PM), Jane, to run it. Jane is going to need some help so Ryan is also going to assign a few junior PMs to the project team.

One of the junior PMs is Aaron. Aaron is very good at the technical side of project management, e.g. mapping out the project plan, monitoring progress, writing reports, etc., but there've been a few complaints from stakeholders about his approach to them. He doesn't really see the need to engage stakeholders or listen to their concerns. He seems to think everyone else loves studying the project plan as much as he does. So he gets very irate with stakeholders who rock up to project meetings without their tasks complete or even knowing that they were supposed to be done. One particular incident blew up pretty spectacularly. Ryan sees potential in Aaron and doesn't want to lose him but reckons that Aaron needs to actively get stakeholders on board with him and his projects if he wants to progress in his career.

Ryan's sense of Aaron is that he brings a very black-and-white approach to project management when it often needs shades of grey. As he reflects more on Aaron's developmental needs, he recognises that Aaron needs to focus on effective stakeholder management; but how do you set an objective to develop *that*?

Aaron needs to increase his ability to identify his key stakeholders, to develop empathy to be able to recognise their various perspectives on the project, recognise power differentials and impact on decision-making and project success. The more Ryan thinks about this, the more he realises that it is quite a complex area to develop competence in. He recognises that there are two parts to it—the first part is the nuts and bolts of stakeholder management, i.e. stakeholder mapping, stakeholder analysis, stakeholder communication, planning, etc. and the second, more complex, part is stakeholder judgement, i.e. how to read situations correctly, anticipate needs, and make the right judgement calls.

Ryan decides that Aaron's initial focus needs to be on building the foundations of stakeholder management and, once mastered, he can set a second follow-on objective, focused on developing stakeholder judgement if necessary. Ryan also recognises that he needs to consider the best way for Aaron to develop the foundations. He identifies several different possible options:

a. Train and coach Aaron himself
b. Assign Jane to train and coach him
c. Get a book on the subject and have him self-learn
d. Get a coach experienced in this area to work with him (could be internal or external)
e. Source a course for him to attend
f. Have him research the topic and present back to Ryan, Jane and/or the rest of the team

As we can see, with a little bit of thought there are numerous ways Ryan and Aaron can approach developing this competency. You have probably already added in an additional option or two that would work for your circumstances. Ryan's initial cut at this objective is as follows:

SMART Objective 13: Effective Stakeholder Management

SPECIFIC: Apply the tools of Stakeholder Management consistently to each assigned project and utilise insights to minimise issues arising

MEASURABLE: Reduce number of stakeholder escalations by 50% (X) and improve project delivery time by 20% (Y)

ATTAINABLE: Yes, tools available

RELEVANT: Minimises project slowdowns due to unhappy stakeholders

TIMEFRAME: *End-month 1:* Source and read relevant articles and/or books and present learnings to team

End-month 2: Apply learnings to assigned SAP project tasks and present to Ryan and Jane for discussion

End-month 3–6: Update Jane on stakeholder management outcomes and discuss any issues or potential concerns. Prepare and present initial stakeholder analysis for any newly assigned projects, as applicable

End-month 7 onwards: Manage stakeholders effectively and keep relevant lead PM in the loop of all relevant stakeholder issues

LEARNING POINTS FROM THIS SMART OBJECTIVE

1. Given that there are many routes to achieving this objective, Ryan doesn't need to have decided on the objective's final roadmap in advance of the objective-setting meeting. While he does need to be fairly clear on what the developmental objective is, i.e. improving stakeholder engagement, and what success would look like, i.e., less issues arising from stakeholders, the route to achieving it can be decided with Aaron during the meeting.

2. However, Ryan does need to consider how much support he is willing and/or able to commit to such an objective prior to the objective-setting meeting. If he doesn't feel he is going to be able to commit to the monthly check-ins, he needs to identify alternatives to how this support can be provided. In this example, he is using a combination of himself and Jane, as the lead PM on the SAP project. An alternative could be that Aaron is assigned a coach and keeps Ryan in the loop through monthly update emails.

3. During the monthly update meetings, scheduled for the end of months three through to six, Jane can assess how well Aaron is developing his understanding of stakeholder management and how well his judgement is developing in relation to reading and understanding the dynamics and the appropriateness of his responses. By starting off with the basics and scheduling monthly meetings to discuss progress, Jane has the opportunity to share her approach to applying stakeholder judgement with Aaron, which he will absorb at his own speed.

4. It is likely that Ryan will seek Jane's views on how Aaron is progressing, what concerns she has about his abilities and, towards review time (or end of project if more appropriate), whether Aaron is fully competent in stakeholder management or if a follow-on objective is required to focus on developing or finessing certain aspects.

5. In such a type of developmental objective, it is very common for managers to just assume that sending the person on a course is the only way to develop the competence. However, this is not the case, for several reasons:

   a. While training courses are very effective and worthwhile, waiting for such a course to be run can be counterproductive. Appropriate online courses may reduce the wait time, but the trade-off may be that the quality and learning might suffer, depending on the quality of the online course.

b. There are alternative ways to obtain the knowledge required, such as books, researching the internet, coaching, etc.

c. It's not just the knowledge that's important here; it's the ability to apply the knowledge to specific situations. Support in applying the learning is as important as obtaining the knowledge.

6. The cadence set out above is monthly, i.e. there is a monthly check-in. Depending on the company and the industry, other cadences, such as daily, weekly, bi-weekly or even quarterly might be more appropriate.

7. The number of periods the objective might cover will depend on the complexity. For example, straightforward stakeholder management might require a few months. It might take someone longer to pick up on all of the nuances of complex stakeholder management in a politically charged organisational culture.

By the time Ryan and Aaron finish the objective-setting meeting, the roadmap could look like any one of the following or some combination:

Table 6: Roadmap Options for Developing Stakeholder Management Skills

	ROADMAP 1	ROADMAP 2	ROADMAP 3
END-MONTH 1	Attend training course & reflect on implications for assigned project(s)	Read book/conduct online research and present learnings to team	Work with coach to understand Stakeholder Management Process & tools
END-MONTH 2	Apply learning to all assigned projects & present insights to Ryan	Apply learning to all assigned projects & discuss insights with Ryan & Jane	Apply learning to SAP project & discuss with Ryan & Jane
END-MONTH 3	Update Jane on stakeholder issues & discuss options	Update Ryan and Jane on stakeholder issues & discuss options	Discuss stakeholder issues & options with coach & implement. Keep Ryan & Jane in the loop

END-MONTH 4	Present outcomes & new stakeholder issues to Jane and recommend two or three possible solutions	Update Ryan & Jane on stakeholder outcomes and new issues & propose solutions	Update coach on outcomes; discuss & explore new issues; agree best solution. Keep Jane in the loop
END-MONTH 5	Present stakeholder issues to Jane & propose solutions for sign-off	Share stakeholder issues, solutions applied & outcomes with Jane	Present issues, outcomes & learning to Ryan and Jane
END-MONTH 6	Update Jane on progress	Update Ryan on progress	Update Ryan & Jane on progress
END-MONTH 7 ONWARDS	Manage stakeholders effectively & keep Ryan in the loop of all relevant stakeholder issues	Manage stakeholders effectively & keep PM(s) in the loop of all relevant stakeholder issues	Manage stakeholders effectively & keep relevant PM lead in the loop of all relevant stakeholder issues

As we can see, including the original roadmap included in SMART Objective 13, there are at least four different valid roadmaps that can be set out for this objective. Some are more costly than others in terms of money and time. Some include wider team learning while others don't. All of them have the following structure:

Table 7: Structure for Designing a Development Objective

STAGE	DESCRIPTION
ACQUISITION OF KNOWLEDGE	Agree how the person will obtain the knowledge & tools & the support needed to succeed
APPLICATION OF KNOWLEDGE	Require applying the knowledge and tools to the assigned projects, tasks or processes
SUPPORT REQUIRED	Consistent support and structure to ensure that time is taken each period to: – review the types of stakeholder issues that arise – consider the nuances and considerations of the various stakeholders – explore possible options to deal with the issues – agree best approach – reflect on outcomes of previous approaches and learn – apply learning to new issues that have arisen

Communication	Mechanism for keeping the manager (Ryan and Jane, for the SAP project) up to date with what is happening and able to provide input into employee's (Aaron) development
Ongoing Expectations	Expectation of when objective should be achieved and incorporated into ongoing performance

The stages outlined in Table 7 can be used as a checklist to ensure that the roadmap for developmental objectives covers all the different elements.

Given how the roadmap is designed (regardless of which option is chosen), unless some underlying issue has not surfaced, Aaron should get to the point whereby he is able to recognise the stakeholder issues and concerns upfront and can design acceptable solutions that deliver the desired project outcomes. Aaron's self-confidence will increase and he will deal with issues on a timelier basis. Ryan, Jane and other PM leads will become confident in Aaron's ability to do so appropriately, reducing their need to get involved or step in.

A key outcome of this objective is an increase in performance due to Aaron being better able to manage stakeholders, reducing:

1. the number of escalated issues
2. the noise and emotion that can arise from poorly managed expectations
3. the amount of time more senior staff (Ryan, manager and Jane, PM, in this case) need to be involved

These outcomes are captured in how this objective will be measured, i.e. reduce the number of stakeholder escalations by 50% (X) and improve project delivery time by 20% (Y).

BEHAVIOURAL EXAMPLE 2: COMMUNICATION

As we saw in Chapter 1, in reality, for most managers it's not the *WHAT* their employees do that drives them to distraction, it's *HOW* they go about it. Over the years, I've noticed that when managers are having a rant about an employee, it's always the way they go about it. My second favourite part of my SMART Objective Setting workshops is when I invite managers to throw out a behavioural example that the group can work through. I never know what kinds of things are going to land. Here's one that Lena offered up:

Lena, from a tech company, shared her experience of an employee, let's call him Riley, who tends to continuously focus on the details of everything and can't see the bigger picture. Anytime Lena tries to have a more general discussion, Riley continuously brings it down a level or two. Lena constantly has to try to lift the conversation out of the detail. If she doesn't nip it in the bud early enough in team meetings, others start engaging with the detail and Lena then finds it very hard to get the team back on track.

This is a great example of someone who struggles to hold discussions and conversations at the right level. They only see one level of conversation, in Riley's case the detailed level, and so don't recognise the need to chunk up or down appropriately.

Here's an example of how such a conversation unfolds during the workshop:

Me:	So, what's going on here with Riley?
Lena:	In every conversation, Riley focuses on the nitty gritty and not the idea. It's very hard to get beyond that with him.
Me:	Okay, so what's the business impact of this?
Lena:	It stalls conversations and takes ages to make a decision. Every time I want to get the team's input and buy-in to something, we end up in these endless discussions and we completely lose the original point. We inevitably run out of time and so the decision gets postponed to the next week. Then I'm under pressure to either make the decision myself or deal with the fallout from my peers for not having made the decision.
Me:	So, it's fair to say that there's a very real business impact from this dynamic. Is Riley aware of this? Have you ever spoken to him about it?
Lena:	No, not directly. I think he picks up on it when I cut him short, but I've never sat down and explicitly discussed it with him.
Me:	Okay, so this objective is something to do with Riley's communication and the need to recognise and hold conversations at appropriate levels. We'll note that down under Specific for

	the moment and come back to it later. Right, moving on to Measurable, what would success look like if Riley succeeded in this objective?
Lena:	Well, the conversation would sound like it is appropriate to the level of the discussion. For example, if we're talking about policy, we're talking about the overall concept of the policy, the purpose of it and not getting into the detail of how such a policy might work in practice. That detail comes later.
Me:	Okay, so conversations are held at appropriate level. What else?
Lena:	Eh, well, conversations would stay on topic. I'm not hearing comments like, "Getting back to the original point," *and* we'd actually get to the end of the conversation with an agreed action point.
Me:	Right, so one measurement would be that action points are agreed and/or decisions made. Anything else?
Lena:	Not that I can think of, at the moment. I'd be delighted if we just got to that point.
Me:	Moving on to Attainable—is this attainable?
Lena:	Well, I don't see why not. Other people can do it.

This is where I might open the floor to the other participants and get their input.

Me:	What do other people think? Is it attainable or might there be constraints of some sort?
Participant 1:	What do other people do within the company? Do they all have conversations at this level of detail or is this more to do with Riley?

This is a really good point to consider. If it turns out that Riley is mirroring the norm in the company's culture, this makes it more difficult to break the habit and also gives insight into why Riley does it.

Lena:	Well, now that you mention it, I do find that other people across the company have a tendency to focus on the nitty gritty. I don't think it's as pronounced, but it could definitely be a factor. I'm only a year in the company so I've been busy getting my head around the job, but it is something I'm starting to notice more and more.
Me:	Great, it's important to know the cultural dynamics that are going to influence this. So, strictly speaking, is this objective attainable? Yes. Will it be easy to slip back to the detail? Yes, so that's going to need to be acknowledged. What type of role does Riley have? What's his educational background? His role within the company?
Lena:	Riley is a software engineer and he works as a programmer.
Me:	So, he's an individual contributor?
Lena:	Yes.

We're starting to build up a picture of Riley. He works in a technical role, focused on "doing". He works in the detail, so he is naturally focused on the detail. When he attends meetings with Lena, his boss, he struggles to recognise that she is less bothered with the detail and more interested in the purpose, or the policy, or the wider process. Most likely, Riley is fairly oblivious to any of Lena's frustrations.

Me:	Okay, he's very focused on the detail, so it's not too surprising that that's where his interest goes during meetings and discussions. If we bring in some of the psychometric models, like Myers-Briggs or Insights Discovery®, would it be fair to say that he's an Introvert Thinking with a preference for Sensing (see Appendix 1 for further detail)?
Lena:	Yeah, he's likely to land somewhere around there.
Me:	Let's move on to Relevance—why does this matter to Riley? Why does he need to be concerned about this?
Lena:	Well, for a start, it's holding him back in his career. I can't send him to talk to an internal client about the project they want

done as he just gets stuck into the minutiae and forgets about what the client is trying to achieve with the project. Even if he does manage to remember what the project is about, the client wonders why they're getting into *so* much detail so early in the project.

Me: Right, so it is important to articulate why Riley might want to engage with this objective. If he's ambitious and wants to progress in his career, this is a skill he really needs to get to grips with.

Lena: Yep.

Me: Is he ambitious?

Lena: I think he is. He's talked to me a few times about wanting to progress and wanting to get involved in high-profile projects. So he is definitely making all the noises about his career.

Me: Great, so we could summarise Relevance as "this is a key skill to become a successful..." what, project manager? Account manager?

Lena: Account manager would be the next step for him.

Me: Okay, so this is a key skill needed to become an account manager. That clearly links the relevance of this objective to his career development. On to Timeframe. For everyone, any thoughts on how we could go about developing this skill?

Participant 1: We could send him on a training course.

Participant 2: Maybe we could get him to read some books or research different communication levels.

Participant 3: After a meeting, Lena could give Riley feedback on how he did and how the conversation could have been refocused at the correct level Lena is looking for.

Participant 4: At the beginning of the meeting, Lena could clearly set out what level the conversation should be at or where the team needs to get to. For example, she could say that she wants to talk about the policy and its purpose, rather than getting into the detail. She could tell them she's going to point out if the discussion is getting too detailed and reset it at the right level. Then, over time, Riley will learn the correct level and that there are different levels of conversation.

As you can see, just like the stakeholder management example, there are numerous ways this could be approached. What often holds managers back is finding the time to tap into their imagination. Even more comforting is that Lena doesn't need to have all of the answers at this stage. She can seek Riley's thoughts and suggestions and incorporate those into the final approach that they agree.

During the workshop, the group typically teases out some suitable plan and puts suitable timeframes around it and identifies likely supports. As we saw in Table 6, we also include an indication as to when Lena expects Riley to be able to hold conversations at the right level and the ongoing expectation that this skill is incorporated into Riley's general performance.

Typically, I then circle back to the Specific and have the group rephrase the objective. Usually, the discussion clarifies what exactly the issue is and so informs what the specific objective needs to be. At the beginning of this discussion, I captured the objective as something to do with Riley's communication and the need to recognise and hold conversations at appropriate levels. So I invite the group to firm up on the final description. Sometimes, they can be substantially different from the original suggestion. For Lena and Riley, a final objective might look something like as follows:

SMART Objective 14: Communication Skills

SPECIFIC:	Consistently contribute to discussions at the appropriate level for both the audience and the purpose of the discussion
MEASURABLE:	Lena not noticing need to redirect Riley's conversation to the right level; Lena not getting similar feedback from others on the detailed focus of Riley's contributions
ATTAINABLE:	Yes, with some coaching and feedback
RELEVANT:	Necessary to develop skill for career progression

TIMEFRAME:

Initially: Agree a word or phrase that Lena and Riley can use to indicate to Riley that he is getting into too much detail

End-month 1: Riley to research, and present to the team, a communication model that highlights the different levels of discussion. Lena to set team expectation to conduct conversations at the appropriate level

Month 2: Riley to identify discussions where he has struggled to recognise the right level of the conversation or to engage at that level of conversation. Meet weekly with Lena to discuss struggles and to gain insight and guidance from Lena

Month 3: Riley to evaluate his own contributions and how he's doing. In conversations where he struggled to identify the right level during the meeting, reflect and offer thoughts and ideas on what might have worked during weekly discussion with Lena

Month 4 onwards: Riley able to contribute at appropriate level. Still able to seek guidance from Lena as needed

LEARNING POINTS FROM THIS SMART OBJECTIVE

SPECIFIC

It is common for managers to start off with a hazy sense of what the performance issue is and, as we work through other parts of the tool and more discussion arises, they become much clearer as to what the specific issue is for their individual employee.

MEASURABLE

How would we measure whether someone is holding conversations at the right level? This is a difficult one. Who is going to measure this? While this is Riley's goal, Lena is really going to be the person who is going to evaluate if he is successful or not. This means, in this case, for the most part, measurement is going to have to focus on evaluating how effectively Riley conducts conversations in Lena's presence. Lena can also seek input from others, if she feels this is appropriate, as she has indicated in this example.

Lena may decide to initially stick to evaluating Riley in the weekly team meetings and, as her confidence in Riley builds, she may invite him to attend a few meetings with other functions or clients and see how he gets on. Along with building her own confidence in him, she is also helping Riley to build his self-confidence. If attending internal/external client meetings is important for his performance, this could also be built into the roadmap.

ATTAINABLE

Is this objective attainable? The immediate assumption is that of course this is attainable. However, as we saw in the conversation above, sometimes there are other dynamics at play that undermine attainability. Acknowledging this and incorporating appropriate responses makes the objective more achievable.

As Lena answers this question, she could realise that it's not just Riley that does this, the whole team does it too but it was just Riley she had consciously picked up on. By reflecting on what is happening, it could transpire that this is actually a whole-team objective and that this is only really going to be attainable through a whole-team change. In this case, she would need to develop the objective in conjunction with the whole team.

RELEVANT

Here's where we discuss the relevance of this objective to Riley's performance. What is the relevance of succeeding in this objective for Riley? As we saw in the conversation above, this objective was relevant for a whole host of reasons. Part of the reason why managers struggle with setting behavioural objectives is the sense or fear that the discussion is too personal. Suggesting that there is a need to set a behavioural objective might be construed as implying that there is "something wrong" with the person. So rather than open that can of worms, the manager soldiers on, being frustrated with the individual, and the team's performance suffers.

When I work with managers on objective setting and performance, to help them depersonalise behaviours, I ask them the following question—*what's the business impact of this behaviour?* Ninety-nine times out of a hundred, they're able to rattle off several reasons why this behaviour is impacting the business. The hundredth time, the answer is likely to focus on the manager's own preferences. Answering this question helps managers see that there is often a very real impact arising from this behaviour.

For Lena, this question centres on whether there are real business impacts from this behaviour or if this is an idiosyncrasy of hers. If her answer is, "Because that's the level of conversation I like having," then setting a performance objective around this is going to cause trouble for her. Why? If Lena can't explain a compelling business reason why this habit is undermining Riley's performance, in all likelihood Riley is not going to buy into this objective so isn't going to put in the effort required to develop the ability to flex his levels of conversation.

Riley's resistance will be subtle. He likely won't come straight out and say he's not accepting the objective. On the surface, it will look like he is acquiescing, but deep down he'll dismiss it as "something to do with Lena" and will ignore it. Reviews will roll around in six or 12 months and both parties will be engaged with some level of subtle conflict as to why it wasn't achieved.

Nobody sets out wanting this scenario to play out, so I always tell managers I'm working with that if they can't put it in terms of business impact, it's not a valid objective to set.

However, in this particular example, Lena has a list of reasons the length of her arm, such as:

- Detailed conversations keep bringing up problems that focus attention away from the discussion and take the team down rabbit holes
- Chunks of meeting time are being wasted
- Team never gets to the end of a discussion so decisions aren't made
- Lack of decisions mean the discussions stay on the agenda week after week
- The same discussions keep being had, week after week
- Lack of decisions means lack of action
- Team's performance is being slowed down by this dynamic
- All this time is being wasted without even understanding if they're the right discussions in the first place, i.e. if they had a broader conversation and decided the theoretical best path forward, then detailed conversations would be more appropriate to figure out the best way to create the path forward

If this particular behavioural example is something you've experienced, feel free to add in your own additional business impacts.

As it happened, Lena decided to contextualise Relevance in terms of Riley's own career. We know Riley is in a very technical programming role and so is very detail-oriented and focused on the tasks, rather than thinking in terms of what the purpose of the details and tasks might be. If he wants to progress in his career, he will need to take a broader view and understand the wider purpose of those details and tasks and how they fit into the bigger picture of the business. By framing this objective in terms of his career, Lena is seeking to tap into Riley's own motivations, increasing his commitment to achieving the objective.

Alternatively, Lena could have used any of the above impacts, or some combination of them, to contextualise the relevance of this objective for Riley. The better she knows Riley and what motivates him, the better insight Lena will have as to the best way to frame this developmental objective for him.

Drawing on Self-Determination Theory, which we will cover in more detail in the next chapter, Riley could have a strong desire to be connected to the group, so framing the objective in terms of the impact on the rest of the team could be an alternative approach. Sometimes it's good to have an initial approach and then one or two alternative approaches in the back pocket, just in case the first approach doesn't resonate.

Unlike with the other types of objectives, where Relevance was framed in terms of an objective's connection to the role, business objectives or organisational strategy, a behavioural objective feels much more personal. So, regardless of how Lena frames this, what is important is that she can link the relevance of this objective to why Riley needs to focus some of his effort on achieving it. He needs to believe that it is in his best interests to succeed in achieving the objective.

When agreeing behavioural developmental objectives, Relevance really needs to tap into the individual's motivations and having an understanding of the Self-Determination Theory can provide insights as to how this might best be done.

TIMEFRAME

As with the Stakeholder Management example, there are several different ways that Lena and Riley may approach developing Riley's ability here and the approach that will finally be agreed ideally should arise out of a two-way discussion between them. Some additional options include:

- Prior to team meetings, Riley and Lena have a pre-meeting to discuss what the level of the conversation should be held at. After the meeting, Lena could give Riley feedback on how he did, give some specific examples of where he became too detailed, explore what a more appropriate level of discussion would have been, and also give examples of where he contributed at the right level.
- As we saw, they could agree a word or phrase that Lena can use during meetings to indicate that Riley is getting too detailed, allowing Lena to reorient the conversation. Riley could note the topic, his preferred level of detail and the reoriented level of the conversation and reflect afterwards.
- They could agree that when Lena sees the conversation slipping down a level (or two), she has permission (i.e. Riley will accept the shift and not have an emotional reaction) to ask questions such as:
  ○ What's that an example of?
  ○ Can we bring it up a level (or two)?
  ○ What's the bigger picture on this?
  ○ Can we leave the detail for a moment and focus on…?
- Lena could give Riley permission to ask her for five to 10 minutes after a meeting to discuss why a level shift had been necessary, to help him understand the different levels of a conversation.
- As suggested, agree that Riley attends some sort of training/coaching session on the Communication Process and Levels of Conversation and presents back to Lena/team his learnings and what he is going to implement.
- Agree that Riley reads a couple of books or researches the topic, creates an implementation plan and agrees it with Lena.

There are numerous different ways that this competency can be developed and the final plan might include several different elements. It also highlights the need for support for Riley to achieve this goal. It would make a huge difference to the team's performance if he did improve in this area, but there's no point in agreeing it if there's no plan as to how Riley can realistically achieve it. As I say to managers, if he knew how to spontaneously change his patterns of thinking and behaving, he would. However, like the rest of us, he can't and so needs support and help to get there.

Lena will need to actively support Riley in guiding him to be able to recognise and conduct conversations at the right level. While this will take some of her time and effort, if achieved, she will benefit hugely, both in terms of the team's performance and the reduction of her own frustration. For a relatively small investment upfront, it is possible for her to reap huge gains. As a manager, it is also part of Lena's role to develop her team.

Another source of support for both Lena and Riley is for them to consider what, if anything, to communicate to the team. Riley's change in behaviour will naturally lead to a change in the team meetings' dynamics that will, most likely, be noticed by the rest of the team. They may also notice that a specific word triggers a shift or a change in conversation dynamics. It could be that they agree that, at the next team meeting, Lena will introduce the general need to conduct conversations at the right level.

If they agree the use of a trigger word or a question, such as "Can we bring it up a level?" Lena needs to consider if she is going to explain to the team that she is going to start using it or if she is just going to start. If she decides to just start using it, she needs to seriously consider how it might be received by the rest of the team.

In reality, the hardest part of this objective is having the initial conversation with Riley to bring it to his attention. Once that's done and Riley accepts the need to develop this ability, it is a case of crafting the most effective roadmap for everyone involved.

In summary, this behaviour is slowing down both Riley's and the whole team's performance due to lack of decision-making and lack of action. If this one change could be made, the whole team's performance would hugely benefit while helping Riley's future career progression.

Before moving on to the next chapter, let's look at one final behavioural objective.

BEHAVIOURAL EXAMPLE 3—NETWORKING

Jane, an experienced project manager in Ryan's IT team, is very good at her job and has potential to take on a more senior role. However, her natural tendency is to hide her talents under a bushel so she doesn't go around telling everyone how wonderful she is. Jane quietly goes about her business, getting things done, sorting out problems, and running projects on time. She is well liked by her colleagues and people who work with her on projects.

Ryan relies heavily on Jane as he knows she'll come through for him. While he'd be more than happy to keep her on his team, he knows that in the longer-term Jane and the company would suffer. Reluctantly, he knows he needs to consider her developmental needs in the context of a more senior role.

Of late, Ryan has mentioned Jane's name to some of his peers and several of them have responded with blank faces or questions of "Jane who?" This concerns Ryan as he knows that the process of Jane getting promoted to the next level will involve input from Ryan's peers and if they don't know who she is, they won't support the promotion. Ryan recognises that Jane needs to increase her internal profile, particularly with Ryan's peers. Knowing Jane, he recognises he will need to frame her development in terms of a stretch goal. He isn't too sure how to approach this, but he takes an initial cut at a SMART objective:

SMART Objective 15: Internal Profile Building

SPECIFIC: Build your internal profile
MEASURABLE: Attend one or two company networking events per month
ATTAINABLE: Yes
RELEVANT: Building network increases profile
TIMEFRAME: Monthly

LEARNING POINTS FROM THIS SMART OBJECTIVE

On the surface of it, this looks like a SMART objective. If I presented this in a workshop and asked participants if it is SMART, they would likely say, "Yes—it's specific, it's measurable and it's time bound; all good solid aspects of a SMART goal. What's not to like?"

SPECIFIC AND MEASURABLE

Is this objective *really* going to deliver the desired outcome? As we have seen in other examples, it would be very easy to succeed in delivering this specific objective and not really achieve the desired outcome of the objective. When Ryan and Jane review it in six months' time, will Jane think she's done an excellent job in this objective while Ryan can't see any change in how his peers view, or don't view, Jane?

If you've ever attended a networking event, you are likely to have seen lots of people *physically* attend the networking event but they're not really *mentally* attending it. They stick to talking to people they know. They strike up a conversation with one person and attach themselves like glue. They chit chat with a few people but never quite bring it around to deepening the relationship.

If effect, it would be very easy to rock up to one or two events a month, chat to a few people, eat some food and leave. Taking a step back and reflecting on what is really going on here, what Ryan means by "networking" is building some level of a relationship with people at his level, i.e. the directors. It means reaching out and building relationships with them, finding commonalities, interests they might have that Jane can contribute ideas to, uncovering their challenges that Jane can help them with, professionally or otherwise, following up with them, and finding ways to build an ongoing relationship of some sort with them. Ryan and his peers know this but, over time, they have migrated to using "networking" as shorthand for all of the above.

So, when Ryan says, "Attend one or two networking events per month," he means make connections with his peers and their top people, find commonalities, uncover business problems they can be helped with, follow up with articles/introductions/suggestions that would be helpful to them, and stay in touch over several months. If effect, Ryan means that Jane needs to ensure she is memorable, in a good way,

What Jane hears is: physically turn up to 1-2 events per month and chat to a few people. With the objective set out as above, Jane could very easily miss the point while still thinking she's doing a good job.

This objective isn't about attending networking events per se; it's about making connections with Ryan's peers, and the people whose opinions they listen to, and building up relationships with them in some tangible way that is going to help Jane stand out and be remembered. So, the number of networking events, while a useful proxy, isn't as important as the number of relevant people Jane connects and follows up with and manages to move towards a follow-up meeting or interaction of some sort.

A more effective Specific might be for Jane to increase her profile with directors and their seconds-in-command. A better Measurement might be "the number of interactions Jane has per month" with this group. One of the routes to creating interaction opportunities might be to attend networking events. Another route could be to seek out and volunteer Jane for projects that would naturally bring her into contact with these people. The final roadmap that Ryan and Jane agree will largely depend on the company's culture, the various acceptable ways people network throughout the organisation, and Jane's own comfort level.

A revised objective for Jane might look like:

SMART Objective 16: Internal Profile Building Revised

SPECIFIC:	Actively build profile with heads of function and their senior managers
MEASURABLE:	Heads of function demonstrate positive response when Ryan mentions Jane
ATTAINABLE:	Should be (see Attainable below)
RELEVANT:	Over time, internal profile with this audience will grow, increasing positive support for future promotion opportunity
TIMEFRAME:	*End-Month 1:* Jane and Ryan to brainstorm suitable ways to create interaction with directors. Agree best options and who is best suited to initiate each option *Monthly Ongoing:* Check-in meeting to discuss profile-building opportunities, progress and name recognition

TIMEFRAME

Looking at Timeframe, we can see that it is being used to initially brainstorm possible ways in which Jane can increase her profile with Ryan's peers and agree a plan as to how Jane can best do this. During the brainstorming session, Ryan might suggest some possibilities that don't sit well with Jane, so she's less likely to follow them through. Some suggestions might require Ryan to put Jane's name forward, so he needs to be happy to do so. Once they have agreed the plan and who needs to initiate what, they both need to execute their agreed tasks.

On a monthly basis, they check in with where things are at, both in terms of Jane's following up on interactions and Ryan's monitoring of whether her profile is increasing with his peers. The monthly check-in can be a quick, "How are things going?" "How are you getting on with Rob?" or, "I was talking to Rob and he mentioned you were going to help his procurement team sort out their IT issue," type conversation or it can be a more formal sit-down-for-30-minutes type check-in.

ATTAINABLE

One point of note with this timeframe is that the roadmap is very short. This objective is based on the assumption that Jane is well able to talk to and interact with heads of function and that, now that it has been brought to her attention, she knows what to do, she's happy to do it and she just needs a bit of support.

This may or may not be true. It could be that Jane doesn't actively put herself into heads of function spaces because she isn't comfortable tooting her own horn or believes that her work should stand for itself, or many other reasons internal to who Jane is. It would be very important that Ryan uncovers any of these possible internal constraints on Jane's thinking during the objective-setting process. If these are a factor, then there would be a need to address them in some shape or form, most likely through assigning Jane a coach, to explore and, possibly, to reframe her beliefs.

Another point on the revised objective is that it no longer specifies how many events Jane should attend. Depending on the individual, it might be prudent to include this.

This objective highlights a very common problem that managers struggle with when setting objectives. They often focus on calling out surface aspects of a goal that tend to be more tangible, as per SMART, rather than the required outcome. While managers' intentions are coming from the right place, i.e. they want their employees to succeed, they often don't take time out to consider the assumptions they are making in relation to both what the purpose of the objective is and the employee's experience and ability to pivot to deliver the goal.

CHAPTER SUMMARY

Behavioural developmental objectives are more complex to design as the drivers of the behaviour can be more difficult to identify. The relevance of a behavioural objective needs to tap into the employee's own motivators; otherwise they are likely to reject the need to put energy into changing their current approach.

In preparing a behavioural development objective, attention should be paid to:

- What the possible drivers behind the current observable behaviour might be, e.g. lack of awareness, lack of knowledge and skills, something deeper that might need a specific intervention.
- What the business impact of this behaviour on performance is—the individual's, the team's, the manager's, the function's, the client's (internal or external) or the organisation as a whole.
- What motivates this person and how the need for them to adjust behaviour and their personal motivations link up.
- What internal constraints might exist for this person, e.g. their beliefs, values, assumptions, etc., that are informing the behavioural patterns that are resulting in the observable outcomes.
- What supports are required to change the observable behaviours.

A final roadmap doesn't need to be firmed up prior to the objective-setting meeting. That will be done during the meeting. However, as we have seen, having clarity around purpose and outcomes, supports, drivers, options etc. helps to design a more effective objective, particularly for behavioural developmental objectives.

PROMPTS FOR YOU:

Identify a behavioural developmental need for one member of your team. Identify the drivers behind this objective need. Consider ways to achieve the following aspects of a roadmap:

- Acquisition of Knowledge
- Application of Knowledge
- Support Required
- Communication
- Ongoing Expectations

CHAPTER 9

The Employee's Perspective

One of the paradoxes of the human that I have always found fascinating is how the same person views pedestrians and drivers depending on whether they are the driver or the pedestrian. For example, when we're a pedestrian, we know we might need the full length of the green man to cross the road, but when we're a driver, we think we can run through a "just-turned" red light because pedestrians don't really need the time. We tend to have less patience as a driver than we do as a pedestrian.

This paradox beautifully highlights how humans can know something in one situation and completely forget it in another. The same paradox regularly arises when we, as the employee, seek to be guided and developed by our manager, as compared to when we, as the manager, perhaps forget our role in guiding and developing our people.

EMPLOYEE'S EXPECTATIONS OF MANAGERS

From the employee's perspective, they naturally look up to their managers as being more senior, more experienced, more successful in having been promoted (at least once), more knowledgeable about how the organisation works, more clued into the role the employee is doing and how it fits into the organisation. By default, the employee typically views the manager as better placed to guide them on what they need to do to also succeed. This is an expectation many employees have about their manager, whether they clearly articulate it or not.

This was brought home to me when I was first promoted from senior fund accountant (SFA) to assistant manager with responsibility of running a team of five. I had been an SFA within a team for about eight months. In case you're wondering, yes, that was a pretty short period of time and not surprising; I was one of the least experienced SFAs. Anyway, on the Friday, I was a peer of all the other SFAs in the equity team, a group that numbered about eight. More importantly, on the Friday, I had been a peer of the SFA of the team I was about to join.

On the Monday, we were working through the work when my new team's SFA came into me and asked me a question about something. I looked at him in amazement that he, who had several years' experience, was asking me, in the *industry* a wet-week, let alone the five hours I was in the new position. He was totally and utterly sincere too. He wasn't trying to make a point; there were no seething emotional undertones to the question. He genuinely was coming to me because he had a question and I was his boss. Logic would have told him that I couldn't have been any better placed to answer the question than him, but his *expectations* told him to ask his manager for direction.

As humans, unmet expectations cause us problems. Even though we may not be consciously aware of our expectations, when they are not met, we start to get irritated, annoyed, frustrated, and disappointed. These emotions start impacting our relationships with those that we sense are responsible for them.

Think of the last time you thought you were going to do something or something was going to happen and it didn't. How did you respond to your expectation? Even something as simple as thinking you're going to a particular restaurant and then finding your table has been given away and you have to go somewhere else can cause a reaction. How long did it take you to readjust your expectations to the actual situation that unfolded? For some people, having to go to another restaurant would ruin their whole evening while others will bounce back after a minute or two.

Even if an employee is aware of their expectations and assumptions of their manager, they are unlikely to share them with their manager. Part of their expectations of their manager is that their manager also knows that part of the manager's job is to develop their employees. This is even more pronounced in social cultures that tend towards the hierarchical, such as the USA, Japan and France.

Just as not getting into the restaurant generated an emotional response, the impact of a manager not meeting these unexpressed assumptions and expectations will generate an emotional response. For many employees, if they continue to remain unmet, the negative emotions will ferment and strengthen, resulting in demotivation, resistance and reduced performance.

SELF-DETERMINATION THEORY

Self-Determination Theory arose from research focused on intrinsic motivators, i.e. motivators that are internal to the individual, as posited by Edward Deci and Richard Ryan (2012). Research shows that people are more likely to succeed in their endeavours when they are internally motivated to achieve them rather than the reward being external, or extrinsic, to them.

In real terms, what this means is that dangling a wad of cash in front of someone who is intrinsically motivated to see if they can master something or not is not going to make them any more motivated. On the other hand, if we keep dangling a wad of cash in front of them, they may become used to the wad of cash and become demotivated when it's removed, even though originally they weren't motivated by the wad of cash. If we dangle a wad of cash in front of people who were never intrinsically motivated to do the task, we will need to continue to dangle the wad of cash to get them to continue to perform.

A very costly mistake organisations and their managers make is to think cash will sort everything out. If something is fundamentally not working in the organisational, functional or team system, throwing cash at it will not solve the problem. It may delay the problem but it won't solve it.

The Self-Determination Theory (SDT) is based on the assumption that people naturally want to develop, grow and master the world around them. For example, as babies hit the six-month mark, they naturally start to want to sit up and move around the place. While they can see parents and siblings walking and moving, nobody is specifically telling the baby they need to start moving around. They just start pushing themselves to see if they can.

The theory also suggests that the surrounding environment plays a part in how this natural tendency develops. A supporting environment allows the natural tendency to flourish while a hostile, negative environment stunts growth and generates a negative mindset. SDT suggests that humans need a sense of autonomy, competence and relatedness to develop and perform in a positive way. It suggests that a lack of these elements leads to demotivation and negative outcomes.

The overarching theory provides six mini-motivational theories that emerged to describe what Deci and Ryan were seeing in their laboratory and field research. We'll take a brief look at each of these and what they mean in terms of objective setting and performance.

1. ***Cognitive Evaluation Theory (CET)*** describes one's intrinsic motivation. It shows up in babies as they push to move through the natural stages of human development. It also shows up in areas such as sport, arts, music, and education. For example, consider any Olympian sportsperson you can think of and consider what motivates them. While they might now be enjoying the extrinsic rewards of succeeding in their sporting domain, it certainly wasn't those extrinsic rewards that got them out of bed at 5:00 a.m. in the morning or saw them training in rain, sleet and snow or pushed them beyond what they thought their limits were. What got them to their sporting peak was their own intrinsic motivation. Many people in the workplace also have this intrinsic motivation and get involved and try things out for the pure satisfaction of challenging themselves and seeing if they can do it. These people look to their managers for guidance on where best to put their effort and to support them in succeeding.

2. ***Organismic Integration Theory (OT)*** examines external motivation. It describes a spectrum of external motivators, some of which are seen by the individual as explicitly external to them, i.e. not part of or connected to them, and so are easily dismissed, and some are seen as adjacent to their internal motivators i.e., if framed in the right way can be internalised by the individual as something they want to achieve. We saw an example of this with Riley and Lena, in relation to Riley's communication skills. If Lena had said the business impact of Riley's communication was that she likes to have high-level conversations, Riley would reject this as a motivator explicitly external to him, i.e. this is Lena's issue, not his. On the other hand, if Lena can demonstrate that this is holding Riley's career back, he may well internalise that and decide that this is something he needs to actively work on.

3. ***Causality Orientations Theory (COT)*** looks at how people read the cultural signs and are motivated to adjust their behaviour accordingly to meet their needs. A person motivated through this lens will see which way the wind is blowing and adjust accordingly, so long as they are getting what they want from it. Perceptions of power and who has it can come into play here, resulting in the person re-prioritising which objectives they're going to focus on in order of which objectives are most likely to meet their needs. Some people are naturally good at reading the cultural signs and adjusting accordingly, for example those with high emotional intelligence. However, other people are less good at it and don't pick up on the cultural cues, so they struggle to recognise the impact of not picking up their performance.

4. ***Basic Psychological Needs Theory (BPNT)*** builds on the human's basic psychological needs of competence, autonomy and relatedness and whether the environment is allowing them to be met or not. So, if objectives can be designed in a way that taps into a person's need for competence, autonomy and relatedness, and the cultural environment in which they will achieve those objectives is supportive, they are more likely to flourish and perform well. If neither the objectives nor the environment supports those psychological needs, people are more likely to start acting in dysfunctional ways. Managers often have an influence on their team's environment and can create the space that allows the team to build on those psychological needs.

5. ***Goal Contents Theory (GCT)*** compares and contrasts intrinsic and extrinsic goals and how those goals impact on a person's motivation and psychological well-being. Research shows that some people actively pursue extrinsic goals, such as wealth and status, rather than intrinsic goals, such as personal growth or close relationships. When setting objectives for someone who is clearly motivated by extrinsic goals, linking Relevance to what they'll personally gain from it is more likely to motivate them to achieve the goal.

6. Finally, ***Relationships Motivation Theory (RMT)*** is an element of the overall theory of self-determination and forms the basis of its own theory, that humans are essentially social beings and desire and need some level of interaction with and closeness to other humans. The theory also suggests that the most effective type of relationship

between humans is one wherein the needs for autonomy and, to a lesser degree, competence are also satisfied.

The objective-setting process itself can either support this motivating factor or undermine it. If a person feels that the objectives are genuinely coming from a place of their best interest, that feeling creates a connection between the employee and their manager that can increase the employee's desire to contribute to the mutual relationship and they are more likely to engage with the objective. Following up with the agreed support further builds on that relationship and trust develops.

On the other hand, if the employee senses that the manager is going through the motions or is thinking of themselves only and not the employee, this undermines and damages the relationship, breaks trust and is likely to result in lower performance and undelivered objectives.

What does SDT mean by competence, autonomy and relatedness? They can be described as follows:

COMPETENCE: being able to learn and master the tasks and process as required to successfully and repeatedly achieve an output or outcome. In effect, it means being able to complete something and not having to depend on someone else to "finish it off" for us or "be corrected". I've worked with several managers who thought that they were doing their team member a "favour" by not going back to them and asking them to correct an error. I can tell you that, while it might be irritating to be corrected, done in the right manner, the sense of satisfaction and increased confidence when they finally master it far outweighs that initial frustration. By not enabling them to master the final bits and pieces, we are actually stunting their growth and holding them back. A good maxim for this element is:

"Give a person a fish, feed them for a day. Teach a person to fish, feed them for life."

AUTONOMY: having a say in how to approach a task or a project, rather than being told and having something imposed. Being told exactly and how to do something feels like micromanagement to many people. Having something "imposed" feels like a lack of control and something happening "to" us rather than happening "with" us. A key factor of success in Change Management is providing people opportunities to input into the solution.

You might well have picked up on the point from the last chapter that, as managers, when designing an objective, we need to be clear on the desired outcome but we don't have to have decided on the final roadmap to deliver the outcome. This is based on a person's need to have some level of input and autonomy about how they might go about achieving the objective. They may identify approaches that would never dawn on you and might be far more effective. They also have a much better sense of where their starting point is. Let's face it; you're trying to figure out their starting point based on observable behaviours. They are much more likely to have a very good idea as to where their real starting point begins.

There is absolutely a need for a manager to take the time to prepare for an objective-setting meeting, particularly around desired outcomes, supports, assumptions, etc.; however, that preparation should *inform* the meeting not *dictate* it. This is about them not you. You gain indirectly by them becoming better able to perform their job.

RELATEDNESS: willing to connect with and care for others. Over the years, I have designed and rolled out performance-management and development processes. As part of the rollout, I provide training to both the managers and the employees. One of the exercises is to break them into groups and ask them to identify the benefits and barriers to effective performance management. A barrier regularly identified by employees is "if you don't really believe your manager" and this barrier goes to the heart of related-ness, motivation and performance.

If you swoop in once a year, set goals and disappear off until it's time to evaluate those goals, your feedback and suggested goals are going to be met with resistance, even if the employee doesn't express it. If you prom-ise support and don't follow through on it, it damages the trust and the relationship, with an all-too-human knock-on effect on performance. Here's the thing—going back to the opening point of this chapter, as an employee we know this; as a manager sometimes we forget.

IMPLICATIONS FOR OBJECTIVE SETTING

Employees both expect and need their managers to provide them with guid-ance as to how they develop, specifically, in their current role, and more broadly, in developing and shaping their career. As we look back over our careers, these are the managers we remember and admire.

Motivation is a complex subject. What motivates one person might not resonate with another. As people's circumstances change, their motivating factors might also change; for example, when a person who typically is intrinsically motivated moves into a new team or company, their need for relatedness may naturally become more important for a period until they feel comfortable with their new colleagues. Another example is the impact of moving into a new life stage; for a period of time, their motivations may shift as they find their way. For example, when someone buys a new house, their external motivator for money may come to the fore for a while.

As a manager, having some level of understanding of a model of motivation and using it as the basis for assessing what a person's possible motivators might be can assist in connecting them to wanting to achieve the objective. In the words of Henry Ford, *"If you think you can, or you think you can't, you're right,"* which beautifully sums up that if a person has the desire and drive to succeed, they will; and if they don't have that desire and drive, they won't succeed, letting themselves, the team, their manager, clients and the organisation as a whole down.

CHAPTER SUMMARY

Being consciously aware of employees' expectations of managers, understanding some theory of motivation, such as Self-Determination Theory, and considering each individual employee's possible motivators can help us to frame objectives in terms that resonate with each employee. The more an employee buys into their objectives, the higher the likelihood that they will put in the required effort and energy to achieve them.

Assuming the objectives have been well designed, the outcome should be increased engagement and performance, along with other benefits such as a high-performing team, a strong succession plan and positive competition for promotions.

PROMPTS FOR YOU:

Reflect on what your expectations of your manager are. Now think about the expectations your team members might have of you as their manager.

Identify one team member and consider what their motivating factors are. Identify where they might fall on the Competence—Autonomy—Relatedness triangle, in Figure 4: Competency-Autonomy- Relatedness Triangle:

Figure 4: Competency—Autonomy—Relatedness Triangle

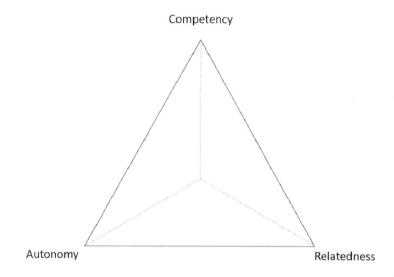

CHAPTER 10

The Manager's Performance Mindset

I don't know about you, but in my experience, most managers groan at the thought of objective-setting time. Reasons for this may include points such as they:

- Find them too time-consuming and don't see any benefits
- Are unclear about how to set objectives
- Don't put the time into preparing for them, making the meeting more difficult and uncomfortable
- See HR as "making them do it"
- Don't see the relationship between objective setting, employee performance and their role as manager
- Have a Telling* leadership style, rather than a Coaching* style, often getting negative reactions

*Telling and Coaching leadership styles refer to specific styles of providing leadership. The Telling style tends towards giving direction and orders without giving context or explanations. The Coaching style tends towards asking questions to bring the person to the point of understanding.

However, as we saw in the examples above, a well-designed SMART objective, with a bit of a helping hand to support the employee in achieving it, can enhance the employee's, the team's and the manager's performance.

Before we take a look at what needs to be done to prepare for objective-setting meetings, and having seen the employee's perspective of objectives, development and the manager's role, it would be good to take a look at the manager's ideal mindset, both towards developing their team and objective setting.

ROLE OF MANAGER

Our role, as managers, is to ensure that the various processes, or segments of processes, under our remit are consistently executed on a timely and accurate basis and that the related outputs and/or outcomes are achieved and delivered to those that need them, be that another function internally, the client or some other external third party. Typically, the amount of work required to be done to achieve all this is more than one person can do in the timeframe. As a result, managers manage a team of people to execute most of the work. The manager's role, then, is to ensure that the team is able to deliver the above, i.e. is able to collectively execute the processes the team is responsible for on a timely and accurate basis.

By extension, part of the manager's role then becomes ensuring that the various different people within the team are able to do their part of the work consistently, accurately and timely. So, part of a manager's role is the need to understand what the purpose of each role within the team is and what the outputs/outcomes are for each role, along with the standards, volumes, competencies, skills, knowledge, developmental path, etc. That goes for the team leader right up to the head of function. It's not that the head of function, with several levels of staff, is going to start getting involved in junior team members. It is to say that the head of function is able to coach and develop his or her direct reports to ensure they are properly developing their direct reports right the way down.

In my experience, when I ask managers what the purpose of the role is (that they are seeking to set an objective for) or what the skills and competencies are, I often get a blank look of "Eh?" It is often the first time they've been asked that question and the first time they've ever thought about it. Part of the role of a manager is to know the parameters of a role and what "good performance" in the role looks like. I think this is a large part of what goes wrong with performance management. There is this expectation that managers just "know" what "good" looks like, from employees, from HR, from the executive team, it's just nobody explicitly told the managers.

So, key to being able to develop a person into a specific role is having a clear vision and understanding of what the end goal of the role looks like. If you're not clear on this, I strongly suggest you take some time out to reflect on what it should look like. If your organisation uses tools such as competency frameworks, it would be worthwhile to review them and extract the relevant elements that apply to the roles within your team. If you don't have access to competency frameworks, review the job description and ask yourself, "What skills and knowledge am I assuming are needed to successfully deliver this role?" Answering that question will provide some insight into what is required.

SEEING PREPARATION TIME AS AN INVESTMENT—IN YOUR EMPLOYEE AND IN YOUR OWN FUTURE CAPACITY

Having managed several teams and having worked with a thousand managers, it's fair to say that most managers tend to be pretty busy with this, that and the other. They are often so busy doing things throughout the year that before they know it objective-setting time has come around *again*. A very common approach to the task is to whisk through it as quickly as possible and get it over with again for another year.

Such an approach is seriously missing a management trick though. Lashing out a few ill-thought-out goals that won't really make a material difference to the employee's performance, the team's performance or the manager's performance isn't much use to anyone involved. Taking such an approach, it's not surprising that most people hate the process.

As we saw in the Introduction, if we view objective setting as a tool of management, designed to actively develop the individual and the team's capability to step up, we get different outcomes. Individuals who improve their performance increase their job satisfaction, their career prospects and their contribution to the team's overall performance. The team collectively delivers more with less conflict, thus increasing camaraderie and reducing staff turnover. In turn, the manager is freed up to take a higher-level view of the team and its purpose within the organisation and identify high-profile opportunities that the manager and the team can participate and benefit from.

A well-selected and well-designed objective, with a clear business case as to why it needs to be delivered, substantially increases the likelihood of it being achieved. Replicate that successful outcome across several employees in your team and you will reap the benefit of investing the time and effort in developing them. If you're new to objective setting and/or you are looking for a more effective way of developing your team, I strongly recommend you take the time to consider and select the top two or three objectives that will really make a difference to each of your employees' performance.

If you commit to giving this approach a try, I can share two insights with you:

a) The first time will take you a while to work through
b) The more times you do it, the easier it will become

As with learning anything new, the first few times will take you a while to work through the steps, but the more times you practise it, the faster it will become. I've done so many that, at this point, I might have the bones of an objective, with a roadmap, sketched out in my head by the time a manager has finished explaining the performance challenge. However, as a trainer and coach, I know it will take me some time to walk the manager through the process. Just like riding a bike or learning to read; the more we do it, the easier it becomes.

OBJECTIVE-SETTING BELIEFS AND ASSUMPTIONS

The work I do, as an executive coach, inevitably focuses on what drives a person's patterns of behaviour. We act off our thoughts and we generate outcomes from our actions. As a coach, once the outcomes and the patterns have been established, the curiosity moves towards the thoughts and what's generating them, i.e. our beliefs and assumptions. As humans, we are often consciously unaware of our beliefs and assumptions, yet they have a huge impact on our lives. By uncovering them and becoming aware of them, we can determine if they are of use to us anymore or if we need to change them.

For our purposes, we'll define a belief as "a view or position that we hold to be true" and an assumption as "elements we assume to be in place without verifying". For example, Lena might hold a belief that "people need to figure things out for themselves", which leads her to assume that because she was able to figure things out for herself everyone else has the capacity to do so too.

If Lena continues with this belief, it will be very difficult for her to prioritise the time she needs to invest in Riley, as the thoughts that will bubble up into her conscious mind will sound something like, *Why can't he figure this out himself? Does he not know how to do this himself? I was able to figure it out, why can't he?* The collective impact of these thoughts will bubble through into Lena's actions via her non-verbal communication, e.g. a slightly curt tone, folded arms, and barely concealed impatience.

Most likely, Riley will sense this impatience and, having his own beliefs and assumptions, will respond accordingly. He may rise to the occasion or he may withdraw, stop asking questions, do his best and fail. The irony, of course, is that if Lena diverted her energy away from those thoughts and channelled it into developing Riley, he'd be performing better and she'd reap the benefits.

While Lena was able to forge her own career to date, based on her belief and innate abilities, in all likelihood this belief is no longer of service to her. As a manager, her mindset needs to shift beyond just herself and into the realm of "What is of service to us, as a team?" A shift of belief to something along the lines of "I am an enabler of the team" or "If the team succeeds, I succeed" would be more beneficial to Lena at this point in her career.

MANAGERS' BELIEFS, ASSUMPTIONS AND EXPECTATIONS

As part of the Introduction, you were asked to answer a series of questions about your beliefs, assumptions and expectations. To finish off this chapter, let's take some time to examine the types of beliefs, assumptions and expectations that support the manager's ideal performance mindset. It's worth your while taking out your original answers, comparing them and seeing if some changes would serve you better going forward. We'll also take a look at how they link to self-determination motivation theory, which we looked at in detail in Chapter 9. As a recap, the questions were:

- What value do you see in objective setting? If no value, what are your reasons?

- What assumptions and beliefs do you have around the objective-setting process?
- Where have these assumptions and beliefs come from?
- In relation to the objective-setting process, what expectations do you have of:
  - You as manager?
  - Employee?
  - HR?
  - The executive team?
  - The organisation as a whole?
- For each group above, are these expectations realistic and appropriate?
- In what ways are these assumptions and expectations currently of use to you?
- In what ways are these assumptions no longer of use to you?

VALUE OF OBJECTIVE SETTING

Seeing some level of value in the process of objective setting is the starting point of the manager's performance mindset. If you don't see any value in it, as per Self-Determination Theory, you're just not going to put the effort in to do it well. If you're struggling with this, think back to the managers that inspired you and the ones that didn't. One of the common factors in managers that inspire is that they help and support their employees navigate their career and give them developmental opportunities. Now ask yourself, "What type of manager do *I* want to be?"

If you don't see value in objective setting, reflect on your reasons as to why this might be. Maybe you've had bad experiences of it. As you have read through this book, maybe you have identified ways in which you unintentionally undermined the process. Maybe you could try out one or two suggestions from the book and see if you get different results.

Done well, setting effective objectives that develop the team's capability results in less overtime, increased motivation, better quality outputs/outcomes, and more opportunities for everyone.

BELIEFS AND ASSUMPTIONS AROUND THE OBJECTIVE-SETTING PROCESS

If you didn't already know, you have most likely gathered that to design objectives well takes effort. It takes time and reflection to diagnose what the real performance issues are or what an employee's next developmental step might be. Our beliefs and assumptions can further undermine the required effort.

For example, a belief such as, "It's sink or swim," informs assumptions such as, "I figured it out so others can figure it out too," or, "If people really want to, they'll figure it out themselves." In turn, these assumptions bubble up into conscious thoughts such as, *Can they not figure this out themselves? Why do I have to waste time on this? Why does HR torture me with this stuff?*

Unless we have put in the work to uncover our beliefs and assumptions, the only part of the above that we have access to is our conscious thoughts. Looking at the set of thoughts above, it is highly unlikely that such a manager is going to spend much time on objective setting, be it diagnosing, designing, planning or conducting meetings. While the manager might think they are gaining time by not investing in these activities, medium-to-long-term they are ironically holding themselves back.

While I have seen managers just put their shoulder to the wheel and put in long hours to get further up the ladder, at some point that strategy no longer works. The cost is also huge, in terms of personal cost, personal life, impact on the team, and impact on the wider organisation.

Reflect on your own answers on your beliefs and assumptions. Determine if they really are of use to you in the longer-term. If you decide they are no longer of use to you, consider what they need to change to. You may need a coach to assist you in making this shift.

SOURCES OF YOUR BELIEFS AND ASSUMPTIONS

It might help you to let go your beliefs and assumptions if you have a sense of where they came from. Often work beliefs and assumptions are shaped by our first real job. If we had a manager that was generous with their time and the environment was very supportive, we are likely to absorb this into our beliefs and assumptions. If we worked in an environment where it was sink or swim, we will think this is the way of the working world. Your beliefs and assumptions may also have been informed by how you were raised or through your school or college ethos.

EXPECTATIONS OF PLAYERS IN THE OBJECTIVE-SETTING PROCESS

It's worthwhile examining your expectations of different groups of people involved in the objective-setting process. Articulating these expectations and considering if they are appropriate or not will help you cultivate the manager's performance mindset.

EXPECTATIONS OF MANAGER

This book has clearly articulated the role of manager in objective setting and development of the team. The manager is expected to have sight of what is required and to ensure the people in each role perform it at the correct level. As managers, they are responsible for actively ensuring that their portion of the organisation is working effectively and aligned to the organisation's purpose. If you identified expectations that don't align with this, it's worthwhile considering how your current expectations are helping or hindering you long-term.

EXPECTATIONS OF EMPLOYEE

The psychological employment contract between an employee and the organisation is that the employee will perform their role to the right standard in return for payment. Implicit in this contract is that the employer will provide the tools, environment, and understanding required for the employee to succeed and that the employee will seek to succeed. The responsibility to provide the tools and understanding and create the environment is delegated to the manager. The expectations of the employee are that they are performing their role, and if not, this is brought to their attention and a plan put in place as to how they can reach that performance. In many organisations, there is also an expectation of long-term career opportunities being made available for employees.

EXPECTATIONS OF HR

In relation to performance, the role of HR is threefold: (1) to provide the performance infrastructure, i.e. to design and make available the performance-management process, policy and templates; (2) to equip managers to use the process, i.e. training; (3) to ensure appropriate and consistent application, i.e. monitor that it is being done consistently across the organisation. HR provides the infrastructure, but, as I say to managers, "Even if there was no HR function, performance management would still be your responsibility." Other than doing so for their own function, it's not HR's role to diagnose performance issues or design objectives for managers. That's up to the managers. If you have expectations of HR over and above these, it might be time to realign them.

If HR aren't delivering the expectations of their role (i.e. providing the infrastructure, training and consistency) then that also needs to be addressed appropriately.

EXPECTATIONS OF THE EXECUTIVE TEAM

The expectations of the executive team are that they should be providing clear direction to the organisation, setting strategy and cascading this down through the organisation. I agree with this expectation. However, in reality, this expectation is regularly not delivered on and unless you are a member of the executive team, you have little to no control over this and limited influence.

A lot of managers use this as an excuse not to engage with the performance-management process. Don't succumb. You are paid to manage, so manage. Don't hold other people's poor management performance as a standard to stoop down to. While you can absolutely justify it to yourself, it reflects really badly on managers that use this excuse, so you will have your own reputational damage to deal with.

For example, if you need to regularly attract people to your project (e.g. consulting or project work), you will struggle to attract the best, increasing the pressure on delivering the project. Another example might be if you need to attract a regular supply of experienced people into your teams (e.g. product design, user experience or client management); the better performers might decide it wouldn't be a good move for them.

Either way, it doesn't help you and your team's performance. Managers that use this excuse reap the negative costs of not investing in developing their team and miss out on the benefits that accrue from actively developing them. We will consider options to best deal with this situation in the next chapter.

EXPECTATION OF THE ORGANISATION

The expectations of the organisation around performance are informed by the organisation's culture in relation to performance and development. If talent development is taken seriously, frameworks such as behavioural competencies, succession plans, etc. are used, and internal promotion is a given, then there is strong likelihood that the organisation expects managers to actively develop team members. Some organisations are so good at this that they prompt gentle rivalry amongst managers to be the manager whose team member is promoted.

On the other hand, if nobody around you invests in developing their people and there's little support in the way of process, training or focus, it's very hard to break the mould. Choosing to go against this cultural norm is is where real leadership shows up. It's about recognising that reasonable expectations of an organisation are not going to be met in this organisation, so the approach needs to be adjusted to the reality and not used as an excuse. It's about having your own vision for your own team, regardless of the unsupportive cultural norms, and executing it anyway.

YOUR REFLECTION INSIGHTS

As you compared your answers to the points above, you most likely obtained some insights into what informs your thoughts and actions, in relation to objective setting, and shed light on the outcomes you obtain from the process. If you don't particularly like the outcomes you're getting and you can see how your thoughts and actions are being informed by unhelpful beliefs, assumptions and expectations, now might be a good time to consider dumping them in favour of more helpful ones.

When working with clients to uncover their beliefs, I'm always fascinated by what happens with an unhelpful belief. Once surfaced, it's like they evaporate into a puff of smoke. We never spend any time designing a new belief, yet the individual is free from the restraints of the unhelpful belief. This isn't just observation. Having noticed the phenomenon, I have asked several people what has happened to the old belief and the response is always, "It's just gone."

Assuming you decide you're going to give this approach a go, the next chapter will help you prepare for an objective meeting.

CHAPTER SUMMARY:

How a manager views objective setting and development is a key determinant to whether they put the time and effort into developing their team members and gain from the resultant benefits. The beliefs, assumptions and expectations a manager holds have a huge bearing on whether they will invest the time or not. It's important to understand what your own assumptions, beliefs and expectations are and consider if they are of use to you or if they are holding you and your team back.

If holding you back, what choices are you going to make to change the outcomes?

PROMPTS FOR YOU:

If you didn't already review your original answers to the Manager's Performance Mindset questions, as part of reading through this chapter, do so now. Ask yourself:

- What needs to change?
- What's your plan to make those changes?
- How are you going to succeed in making those changes?

CHAPTER 11

Preparing for SMART Objective-Setting Meetings

A core reason to set objectives in the first place is to increase the likelihood of the required performance outcomes being realised. This is achieved by the objectives being well-designed and appealing to the employee's motivations.

To effectively appeal to an employee's motivations, a well-designed objective needs to start from the right point; however, we often don't know what the right starting point is or their motivators. We need to uncover what both of these are during the objective-setting meeting, but we can't go into that meeting blind.

So, the purpose of preparing for the objective-setting meeting is to:

1. Identify the required performance outcomes that will make a difference.
2. Identify the potential drivers and the possible starting points.
3. Consider what the employee's possible motivators are.

To support all of this, we also need to identify the potential constraints and supports required so that during the meeting we can agree realistic objectives that really can be attained. Ensuring we don't go into these meetings blind requires quite a bit of consideration and preparation. However, as promised earlier, the more we practice this approach, the easier and faster it gets.

By the end of the objective-setting meeting, the aim is to agree four to six final objectives. One to two of these will be informed by the business needs and one to two by the functional or team needs. Another one is likely to be purely developmental and one, maybe two, will come from the individual themselves.

When preparing for an objective-setting meeting, it's helpful to identify a list of seven to eight possible objectives. These can then be whittled down to a shortlist of five to six objectives, all of which you'd be happy to include in the final agreed set. The final set will be agreed during the meeting.

So, how best can a manager prepare for an objective-setting meeting? Let's take a look at what needs to be considered in advance of the meeting.

10 STEPS TO SMART OBJECTIVES PREPARATION

1. Current Performance Assessment
2. Core & Secondary Objective Type(s)
3. Objective Drivers
4. Business Impact
5. Objective Purpose
6. Roadmap Options
7. Potential Constraints
8. Potential Supports Required
9. Link to Motivations
10. Objective Categorisation

We've covered a lot of different ideas over the course of the book so far. This chapter guides us on how to bring it all into one place in preparing for an objective-setting meeting. If you haven't already done so but would like to, click here to access your free SMART Objective-Setting Meeting Preparation Template, or go to http://bit.ly/SMARTFreeGifts, to download it.

As you are reading through this chapter, it might be helpful to identify one person in your team and apply the content to them.

1. CURRENT PERFORMANCE ASSESSMENT

When considering objectives, it's helpful to clarify where you see the individual's current performance level for each potential objective. To assess their current level, think about their performance in relation to their current job by asking yourself the following questions, noting down your answers in the roughwork section:

a) Are they relatively new to the role, so are they are still in learning mode? If so, what key tasks, outputs, outcomes do they need to master in order to be able to perform their role effectively? If so, go to Still Learning.

b) Have they been doing the role for a while and are able to do the main tasks/outputs/outcomes of the role but let themselves down in one or two areas? Note down these areas and go to Performance Issues.

c) Are they a solid performer, able to do all aspects of the role? What would their next development step be? How can they contribute further? If so, go to Good Performer.

d) Is this a high performer who is ready for the next level and needs to be stretched? What are two or three appropriate areas to stretch them? Note down these areas and go to High Performer.

STILL LEARNING: Rank the key tasks/outputs/outcomes of the role in terms of which are most important to mastering the role; evaluate where the individual is on each task and prioritise setting objectives focused on the highest-ranking ones that they haven't already mastered in full.

PERFORMANCE ISSUES: For most managers, this is where they spend the majority of their performance-management focus. As we saw with Riley and Aaron, understanding the drivers behind these performance issues will shed light on how best to construct appropriate objectives and support the individual. See section 4, Objective Drivers, for further tips on how to surface and articulate performance issues.

GOOD PERFORMER: In this case, the individual is well able to deliver the outputs and outcomes of the role and their performance is where it should be. Consider what you think the person is capable of achieving, particularly in relation to business-aligned objectives, and what they would need to do to get there. If you haven't already done so, a well-timed chat with the person about their career ambitions is appropriate.

HIGH PERFORMER: If there's an obvious career path, consider what the step-up to the next level is, where this person's gaps are and identify one to two areas they can start focusing in on to prepare them for the next level. If there is no clear career path, and you haven't already done so, a serious career-ambitions chat will need to be had to identify the most appropriate next step for them.

As managers, having sight of the context of the objective helps us frame the objective for the individual. For example, when someone is still learning their role, hearing that they are doing well, that they're on the right track to achieving the required standards and here's what they need to do to finesse their performance will lead to their being more receptive and positive towards those objectives. The alternative, of having the same objective set in a vacuum, affords them the opportunity to fill in the context and they may or may not fill it in correctly.

Remember, they have their own beliefs and assumptions that you, as their manager, are unlikely to be aware of. So, if they decide to contextualise the objective as evidence that they clearly aren't doing a good job, they will perceive the process as negative and demotivating.

From this analysis, identify a list of possible objectives arising from the employee's current performance in their role. Layer in possible functional and/or business-aligned objective areas and identify aspects or elements that are appropriate for this person.

In effect, this is what Jenny did when Rob told her about the SAP project. She recognised that Ray would benefit from developing his project-management skills and the business-aligned SAP objective was a great opportunity for him to practise them.

As we saw in the previous chapter, many managers raise concerns about not having sight of the business strategy or even their own objectives. A common question arising from this is, "How can I allocate objectives appropriately across my team if I don't know what my own are?" If you find yourself in this situation, there are several options, as follows:

1. Option one is to consider what business-aligned objectives are most likely to come down the tracks and use those. If they turn out to be wildly different when you do finally get sight of them, you always have the opportunity to set up a follow-up meeting two or three months later and change the objectives at that point.
2. Option two is to get a sense of the types of functional initiatives that are likely to be focused on during the period and use these.
3. Option three is, as manager, to identify the projects or changes you want your team to achieve and use these. There are always improvements that can be made that ultimately help the team, function and business improve.

Once completed, you should have a long-list of seven or eight possible objectives. The accompanying template has space for eight potential objectives, split into 4 x 2 tables. We will use these as the basis of evaluating each of them further and creating that final shortlist of objectives you want to bring to the objective-setting meeting.

2. CORE AND SECONDARY OBJECTIVE TYPES

As introduced in Chapter 1 and covered in detail in Chapters 5, 6, 7, and 8, as part of preparation it's good to be clear on what type of objectives are being proposed and if they are appropriate for the individual. For example, for someone who is still learning their role, their objectives are more likely to be role-specific. For a high performer, they are more likely to be business-aligned.

As noted earlier, some objectives might straddle two types of objectives, e.g. business-aligned and developmental. It's good to be clear if an objective touches two types. In my experience, while the manager might recognise that an objective is both organisationally and developmentally driven, oftentimes employees are less clear. This lack of clarity might lead them to conclude that their objectives are only focused on the business and not their needs.

Building on what we learnt about Self-Determination Theory, if people can see how mastery of a competency results in their autonomy, they are much more likely to commit the energy required to succeed in the objective.

3. OBJECTIVE DRIVERS

As we saw in Chapter 4, objective drivers are the drivers behind why a specific objective is being set. It links to the objective type, e.g. business-alignment or developmental. It also links to the individual's current level of performance. For many of these combinations, the objective drivers will be fairly obvious. For example, the driver behind a "High Performer" and a Business-aligned objective is to give them the opportunity to broaden their understanding and network and increase their profile while representing the team. The longer-term aim is to prepare them for other opportunities, be that a promotion or a move to another area.

Similarly, the drivers behind a "Solid Performer" and a Role-specific objective type might be to broaden their experience and understanding of their current role and deepen the team's bench-strength.

However, for those individuals who fall into the "Performance Issues" category, the driver is often hazier, as we saw with Riley and Aaron. To help us better identify these objective drivers let's take a deeper look at what might be undermining these individuals' performance.

UNCOVERING POTENTIAL DRIVERS FOR PERFORMANCE ISSUES

On occasion, I'm asked about how to best deal with a high performer, but for most managers, their main challenge with performance management and, by extension, objective setting is working with employees with performance issues. This is where most of a manager's performance-management time is spent.

For these employees, use the SMART Objective Setting Performance Issues Driver Analysis Template (click here to access or go to http://bit.ly/ SMARTFreeGifts to download) or on a sheet of blank paper note down the specific performance issues that you are aware of. If it helps, think of specific situations and sketch out a brief outline of the observable behaviours. Then ask yourself the following:

- What is this (are these) an example of?

For instance, someone keeps coming over to you with a problem and you think they should be able to answer it themselves (and/or it's just driving you nuts!). What is this an example of?

- Are they lacking in confidence?
- Are they afraid to make a decision?
- Do they not know enough to be able to make a decision?

Another example might be someone who is never prepared for meetings. The observable behaviours include: always last to arrive; they never read the meeting papers circulated prior to the meeting; and they regularly ask questions that indicate they're not following the conversation. What is this an example of?

- Lack of time management and/or organisational skills?
- Lack of interest?
- Someone who is covering out two jobs, while a colleague has gone on extended leave, and is constantly chasing their tail?
- Someone who constantly volunteers to get involved in projects and has overextended themselves?
- Someone who is out of their depth or new to their role?

As the saying goes, "eaten bread is soon forgotten", which neatly highlights the "recency bias" (the phenomenon whereby a person remembers something that happens recently as compared to remembering something that may have occurred a while back) that humans are prone to. When it comes to performance and objective setting, managers are so busy that it is very easy for the recency bias to kick in and they only focus on what has been going on in recent weeks rather than taking a longer view.

As an aside, this recency bias is also why most performance-management processes seek to encourage regular check-ins and brief note-taking throughout the year. It is to ensure that performance evaluation is based on the whole period and not just the last couple of weeks or months.

When assessing performance standards and related developmental objectives, it's important to consider what is really going on and not just consider the recent evidence. If we take the example of the poor meeting focus, has this person always been like this or, as some of the possibilities above point to, has something happened to their workload or the type of work they are doing that has resulted in this noticeable change of behaviour?

Trying to set an objective in an area that is a result of the person being so overstretched or out of their depth, due to a new position or an absent colleague, could potentially generate a lot of unnecessary animosity and demotivation.

In some instances, it is worthwhile asking the question, "What is this an example of?" several times, each time taking the answer up a level. For example:

Level 1: What is this an example of?
- They're not very organised

Level 2: What is that an example of?
- They're not prioritising preparation for the meeting

Level 3: What is that an example of?
- They're reflecting how they see other people turn up to the meeting (i.e. this is a meeting culture issue)
  Or
- They don't see the importance of being prepared and how it influences how they are being seen by managers from other departments (i.e. this is a stakeholder management and influencing issue)
  Or
- They don't have the time because Carrie is on extended leave, so they're covering Carrie's role on top of their own (i.e. this is a resourcing issue)

Asking the question a few times helps us to better understand what the real performance issue is. In this case, by asking the same question three times, we could get to three very different answers. The second answer is within the employee's control to do something about. It is possible for them to change their level of self-awareness and develop the skills and understanding to better manage stakeholders.

The other two options, meeting culture and resourcing, are less likely to be in their control. In the first option, if there is a wide-scale need to overhaul the meeting culture, this objective would need to be set against a backdrop of everyone in the team or function being assigned an objective focused on the required culture shift. In the third option, this could be a short-term concern, so best to ignore. If Carrie is going to be out for a few months, the resourcing issue needs to be sorted out appropriately, for example by getting a temporary replacement for Carrie; splitting out the work across the team; or reallocating some of your employee's work so they can take on more of the load arising from Carrie's role.

Again, setting and holding an individual to an objective that is beyond their control is likely to generate unnecessary animosity as they might feel that they are being set up to fail. Linking it back to Self-Determination Theory, they may feel that they don't have autonomy in this objective as it is dependent on others adjusting their behaviours too. If persisting with such an objective, it would be very important to highlight and discuss what is attainable and within their control and what is outside of their control and ensure this is appropriately captured in the final objective.

For example, while it is not possible for the individual employee to ensure that everyone else in the meeting has done the pre-reading, what is in their control is that they turn up to meetings on time; come prepared, having read and considered the pre-reading; and ask questions that show they are following the discussion. Such an objective might look like:

SMART Objective 17: Increase Meeting Effectiveness

SPECIFIC:	Increase meeting presence and impact
MEASURABLE:	Arrive on time, fully prepared (pre-reading, considered points, etc.), and actively and effectively contribute to discussions
ATTAINABLE:	Yes, all within own sphere of control
RELEVANT:	Need to improve presence in front of stakeholders
TIMEFRAME:	Ongoing, starting immediately

In this particular example, there's no need for a roadmap to be included under Timeframe, as it's fairly straightforward and can be implemented immediately. It's more a case of setting out what the expectations are, as indicated in Measurable.

4. BUSINESS IMPACT

As we saw in Chapter 8, it's important to understand why focusing on this specific objective matters. Putting it in terms of business impact is important, both in terms of depersonalising the objective and for building credibility. The business impact for some objective types is easier to articulate—it's linked to the business strategy or the purpose of the specific role and how it supports other roles, functions and/or the client.

With behavioural developmental objectives, particularly those identified for someone considered to have performance issues, putting the objective in terms of business impact can be more difficult. However, not putting it in terms of business impact can lead to an individual dismissing the objective as irrelevant to them.

In addition, since performance management has become synonymous with bonuses and pay rises in a lot of companies, this becomes even more important. If Riley knows he's going to get more or less the same bonus if he delivers the objective as if he doesn't, there isn't much motivation to put in the required effort to achieve it. He needs to see how achieving this objective is going to help him in the medium-to-long-term and tap into his desire for competence, autonomy and relatedness.

Building on Levels 1–3 outlined in Section 3: Objective Drivers, we could add in a Level 4 and ask, "Why does this matter?" Put another way, what is the business impact of this? So, between Objective Drivers and Business Impact, we can ask a series of questions, as follows:

OBSERVABLE BEHAVIOUR:

Ill-prepared for meetings, e.g. turns up late, asks questions that indicates they haven't read the pre-reading, etc.

LEVEL 1:	What is this an example of?	Lack of organisation
LEVEL 2:	What is *this* an example of?	Not prioritising meeting preparation
LEVEL 3:	What is *this* an example of?	Doesn't recognise impression being given
LEVEL 4:	What is the business impact of this?	Lack of influence on stakeholders

Note the difference between Drivers and Business Impact. A driver is something that is influencing and driving the need for the objective. Some drivers, such as business strategy and job specific, are impersonal by their nature. Other drivers, such as behaviour developmental, are very personal by their nature. It is vitally important that these are put into the more impersonal terms of their business impact.

On the other hand, business impacts trend towards the impersonal and focus on the desired outcomes the business needs to achieve.

5. OBJECTIVE PURPOSE

As we saw in Chapter 4, managers often start off saying that the objective is about X, but by the time we work through the process, they have concluded that it is actually about Y. It is very common for managers to focus on the surface behaviour and agree an objective based on that rather than digging into the impact of the surface behaviour and articulating the real performance or development gap.

Surfacing both the drivers and the business impact should help to articulate what the real purpose of the objective is, which, in turn, helps shape the final objective. As the purpose of each of the proposed objectives becomes clear, it may turn out that some potential objectives are parts of other objectives and can be combined.

Remember, the Objective Purpose captures the desired output or outcome, if the individual takes on responsibility for delivering it and not just a step along the way, e.g. training or running the project. As we saw, an objective isn't "running the project" or "attending the training", it's the outputs or outcomes of having run the project or attended the training successfully.

If you suspect the objective will run over two performance periods, the purpose is still the output or outcome, with an acknowledgement of where the project should have progressed to by the end of performance period one.

6. ROADMAP OPTIONS

At this point, we have a good sense of where our starting point A (employee's current performance and drivers) and ending point B (objective purpose) are for this particular objective for this particular individual. That allows us to sketch out a few options as to how we can get from A to B and what the possible milestones might be along the way.

While you own the ending point B, i.e. it is mostly your vision of what the purpose of the objective is and what success looks like, you don't have full sight of the starting point A. So, at this point, it's only possible to have an idea of what the roadmap might look like as it is very likely to be adjusted during the meeting. However, it does give you some sense of the possible routes available.

Once the constraints and supports have be reviewed and considered, several further options may be identified and added to the list.

7. POTENTIAL OBJECTIVE CONSTRAINTS

As we saw in Chapter 3, constraints may exist that our assumptions cause us to overlook. Taking time to consider what assumptions we're making and what constraints may actually exist help us to surface possible issues that might undermine the employee's ability to succeed in the objective.

For example, the assumptions we make in relation to objective drivers might throw up some constraints. In the case of preparing for meetings by having read through the materials, the employee may have dyslexia, which is likely to be a huge part of why they haven't done the pre-reading. No amount of asking them to devote more time to the pre-reading is going to remove the impact of the dyslexia. Finding alternative ways, such as converting it into a voice memo that they can listen to in order to access the knowledge would be a much more effective way to minimise this constraint. It may turn out that others find these alternative methods more beneficial too.

In reality, you may not have sight of all the constraints that might exist. The employee might have sight of constraints that your own experiences, assumptions, beliefs and expectations prevent you from seeing. In turn, something you might see as a potential constraint might not be an issue for the employee. The purpose of identifying some potential constraints is to be able to raise the topic at the meeting and have an example or two to get the conversation going.

8. POTENTIAL SUPPORTS REQUIRED

Following on from potential constraints, it's a good idea to identify potential supports that might be needed and how they might be extended. As we saw in Chapter 7, support often comes in the shape of a training course, but there are many other ways it can be extended. It could be through coaching, on-the-job training, shadowing someone else, being assigned a mentor, being volunteered for a project, signing off on a plan, or lots of other ways.

Identifying some of the types of support that might be required, the resources, such as time and money, that might need to be invested, and thinking about who might be best positioned to provide such support will help frame the objective discussion at the meeting. There is no point agreeing to supports that you know won't or can't be followed through. As we saw earlier, viable support options will also be informed by organisational constraints such as training and coaching budgets.

NOTE ON WHEN "SUPPORT REQUIRED" BECOMES A CONSTRAINT

It is important to ensure that a required support doesn't become a constraint to achieving the objective, i.e. a support that, as it wasn't provided, meant the objective became unattainable.

Along with providing training to managers, I also provide performance training to employees, so I have pretty good insight into their concerns on objective setting and reviews as well. Here's a very typical example of a conversation around support:

Me: Okay, so you've agreed the objective roadmap and, as we can see, one of the steps is that you'll need to agree the plan you develop with your manager.

Employee: But how will I get my manager to agree the plan?

Me: Well, you'll need to set up a time with them and ask them.

Employee: Yeah, I'm not sure that's going to happen. They're forever cancelling meetings with me.

Me: In that case, I'd suggest that you reschedule it a few times.

Employee: I've tried that before with other stuff and it never works. How many times should I try?

Me: Em, thinking about it, I'd suggest you try to reschedule four or five times. I think that's reasonable. However, if you think this is going to be an issue and that the plan is never actually going to be agreed, then I'd suggest that, when agreeing to this objective, you discuss the need for the sign-off meeting to go ahead and to ask for direction around what to do in the event it keeps getting cancelled. I also suggest that you keep note of the times you requested or scheduled the meeting, when it was postponed and by who. So, when it comes to the end of the review period and it turns out it wasn't done, you can highlight the reasons why. If you have an interim one-to-one meeting, you could also share these insights at that meeting too.

Employee: Okay, that makes sense.

Me: This really is a question about trying to figure out the line between taking responsibility for sorting out getting access to the support you need to succeed in the objective and how far you can push before it becomes someone else's performance issue. So, asking once or twice wouldn't be considered pushing hard enough, but if you've tried five, six, or even seven times, then it's reasonable to assume that it's no longer your performance issue.

Employees are often stuck in a catch-22 situation. They might need support of some sort or another from their manager, the organisation or the team, but they're not sure how to go about getting it. They want to know what sorts of support they can expect from their manager and many will want direction on what they should do in the event that the support isn't forthcoming. What they're looking for is permission to raise the lack of support with their manager and a sense of how many times they can raise it and it will still be okay. While employees can ask for this guidance and support, it's not particularly pleasant for them to feel that they are being put into the situation of having to ask.

For example, I worked with a professional services organisation where the partners were constantly busy. They wanted their people to succeed but were often too busy to give their employees time. During the objective-setting meetings, it became a recurring theme to hear the partner say, "Please, keep at me until I do it. I know I'm very busy, but this is important so I'm fine with you keeping after me." That gave the employees a lot of comfort to know (a) it's nothing personal, the partner is just busy; and (b) nagging is good.

To be fair to those partners, they did really mean this. They definitely rated those employees that nagged until something was done more highly than those that asked once. My point here is that when those partners said that, they meant it. If you say it and you don't mean it, it will become apparent very, very quickly and you'll have a credibility and trust issue, which sounds something like this:

Employee:	So, what happens if the sign-off meeting to approve the plan doesn't happen?
Manager:	Well, if that happens, I give you full permission to keep after me and reschedule it.
Employee:	Really?
Employee's head:	*Yeah, right. Last time I kept on at you to sign off on a project, you snapped at me and told me to just go ahead and do it. Then, when it was done, you hated i, because you hadn't looked at the proposed plan and it had to be redone.*

People are not stupid. Once bitten, twice shy. If you're not going to follow through on a certain type of support, don't promise it. If support is the difference between succeeding and failing in this objective, then it's important to figure out how that support is really going to be provided; hence the need to figure out the various options to deliver on the objective. Is there an alternative way to deliver this objective without the type of support that you're not in a position to give? Are there alternative ways of providing support that you can follow through on? For example, can you assign someone who has both the capability and the capacity to provide the support?

If you're reading this, thinking, *There's a possibility that this may be true of me,* or, *Some people might say that about me,* then I strongly suggest that you reflect on whether, on the whole, the constraint around support is working for you and your team.

If you decide that promising support and not following through on it is not particularly useful, you can choose to acknowledge the possibility that such constraints around support might arise upfront with team members, either on a one-to-one basis or in a team meeting. This makes it a lot easier for the employee to bring up the conversation further down the line. Again, the better they succeed, the better you succeed and you may even find that you have bought back some of your own time as their performance increases.

Once the constraints and supports have been identified, it's worthwhile going back to the Roadmap Options section to capture any additional options that have surfaced.

9. LINK TO MOTIVATION

Before being able to decide on the final list of objectives, it's worth taking a couple of minutes to link this proposed objective to the individual's possible motivators. Take some time to identify what you think motivates them. Examples include: being able to do their job without being directed the whole time; the possibility of a promotion; contributing to the development and support of team members.

Uncovering their motivations provides insights in two useful ways:

- If we identified six to eight plus possible objectives that we are looking to narrow down to five to six, objectives that are more naturally aligned with the employee's personal motivations are more likely to be achieved. We can use this insight to select the final set of proposed objectives.
- Having a sense of their motivations for each objective helps us frame the objectives in terms that resonate with them, increasing the likelihood of buy-in to delivering the objectives.

10. OBJECTIVE DECISION

Having evaluated the potential objectives, the final step in this preparation process is to decide which to include in the final shortlist using the following categorisation:

- Must Do
- Optional
- Hold Over
- Reject

MUST DO: Objectives that end up in this category are ones that definitely need to be included in the final set of objectives agreed. They are likely to have a strong connection to role-specific and business-aligned objective types. A behavioural developmental objective type might also find its way into this category if the demonstrated behaviour is particularly detracting from performance.

OPTIONAL: These are objectives that, if there is room, can be included but they're not make-or-break to the individual's performance. For employees whose performance falls into "Solid Performer" and "High Performer", they are likely to be objectives that add the finesse to their performance or stretch them. For employees whose performance falls into the "Still Learning" and "Performance Issues" categories, they are likely to cover development areas that do need to be included at some point but are not the most pressing. These can be categorised here or in the Hold Over category.

HOLD OVER: Objectives that fall into this category are ones that could be held over to the next period. An example is a follow-up objective to one set in this performance period. Using Aaron's stakeholder management objective, we had identified two possible aspects to it. The first was understanding the tools of stakeholder management, and how to apply them to analysing stakeholders. The second was the softer side of stakeholder judgement. In this case, the first aspect could be a Must Do objective while the second could be a Hold Over, to be assessed in the next performance review period and possibly assigned at that point.

As we saw above, some objectives identified as Optional may also be Hold Over. These can be reassessed in the next review period and determined if they're still relevant at that point.

REJECT: Objectives in this category are those that, upon reflection, are not relevant objectives. Examples might include thinking that the issue is X and realising that it's been captured as part of a Y objective or realising that, like the meeting's culture, the issue is broader than the individual and needs to be addressed with a different approach. It could be rejected due to a lack of clear business impacts or because it is evident that the individual's motivations are unlikely to support it.

CHAPTER SUMMARY

At this point, you have a list of possible objectives with a good idea of why each of them matters, how to frame each of them with the employee, possible routes to achieving them and the supports required to enable the employee to successfully achieve them. They have also been categorised into those that definitely need to be included and others that are optional and/or can be held over.

Typically, between four to six objectives will be agreed, three to four coming from management and one, maybe two, coming from the employee. If your organisation's performance cycle is six-monthly, i.e. objectives are set every six months (not just reviewed as part of a check-in), then this number would likely be revised down. Adjusting the number of objectives set would also be appropriate for other performance cycle durations.

Encouraging the employee to add in an objective that they would specifically like to achieve taps into the human's need for some level of control and autonomy; the objective they set may or may not dovetail with one of the objectives you had identified, and that's okay.

Once you have identified your shortlist of objectives, this is the list that you, as manager, will bring to the objective-setting conversation and keep in your back pocket. It is a list of objectives that you'd be happy to agree to while recognising that one or two probably won't be included in the final set of objectives agreed at the meeting. These will form the basis for your objective-setting meeting.

CHAPTER 12

Conducting SMART Objective-Setting Meetings

As explained in the Introduction, this book is only focused on the process of objective setting and does not seek to touch on other elements of the performance-management process, such as how to give effective feedback. Some organisations split out performance review feedback and objective setting into two separate meetings while others merge the two stages into one meeting.

There is merit in both approaches and, as with everything in life, there are pros and cons to both. If your organisation separates them into two meetings, then this chapter is focused on the second objective-setting meeting. If your organisation merges them into one meeting, as explained in the Introduction, this book is only focused on the objective-setting aspect and so you will need to prepare for the feedback element separately albeit the objective-setting preparation may well inform the performance evaluation and feedback aspect.

Recapping on the real purpose of SMART, it's a tool that allows manager and employee to have a real, two-way and detailed discussion about what an objective really means within the context of their role, their career, the team, the function and the organisation. A desired outcome is that the employee buys into the objective and commits the effort to achieving it. With this in mind, let's look at how we can support this during the objective-setting meeting.

OPENING THE OBJECTIVE-SETTING MEETING

Whether it's part of the one meeting or its own separate meeting, open this conversation by giving an overview of what the meeting will cover, the expected outcomes (i.e. we'll have a solid set of objectives), your role and that of the employee in the meeting, and the expectations about input and discussion.

The meeting opening can also include the preparation you've done and how that will be used, i.e. it will form the basis for the starting point for the discussion. If the employee is relatively new to the organisation, or if SMART has been recently introduced, check in with them to see what they already know about SMART and follow up with explaining your understanding of and approach to SMART.

Finish off the opening by inviting them to clarify points, ask questions and share their thoughts on the proposed approach and answer accordingly.

BROAD INTRODUCTION OF OBJECTIVES

Provide a broad overview of what you're hoping to achieve by setting the identified objectives and link back to the performance review evaluation and feedback stage or meeting. You can also touch briefly on relevant preparation work you feel appropriate to share, if not covered in the opening. As you start to move on to exploring the first objective, you can invite them to select where they'd like to start, as this signals interest in their participation.

EXPLORING SPECIFIC OBJECTIVES

At this point, the conversation is moving into the nitty gritty of discussing and agreeing each objective and putting it into the SMART format. Share your understanding of what you see as the purpose of the objective and invite their thoughts on it and issues or concerns they might have with it.

Move on to how this might be measured and discuss the different options, shortcomings and strengths of each and narrow it down to one or two measures. These might change as the conversation progresses and its okay to indicate this. It demonstrates that the process is fluid and the employee does have a very real input into the final objective agreed, rather than feeling that it's being imposed on them.

Ask questions to explore where they see their starting point. If you have seen evidence to suggest that you feel their starting point is elsewhere, ask questions to prompt their awareness, share examples to highlight where you think the starting point might be, invite them to reflect on the examples and explore their insights. Between the two of you, you'll likely hit on a good starting point.

If you feel the person isn't fully ready to admit where their real starting point is, I suggest you don't get into a stand-up row with them. It's more important that (a) they've agreed that an objective in this area is necessary; and (b) you start somewhere. This situation is most likely to arise in behavioural developmental type objectives, but don't discount it showing up in other types of objectives too.

Like we saw with the example of Aaron and the starting point on stakeholder management, it may well be that you start with the technical aspects of the topic, which by definition are less personal than a person's style and approach. For Aaron, it was focusing on the technical aspects of stakeholder analysis and creating and implementing a communication plan. Remember, you still have the opportunity to evaluate the outcomes of the technically-focused objective in the next objective-setting period.

If it turns out that performance in this area is still an issue, you can always revisit it, knowing that you've taken the technical aspects off the table. In Aaron's case, he would no longer be able to say he doesn't understand what stakeholder management is. At this point, you could delve deeper into some of the potential issues that you suspect might really be undermining their performance while there are less excuses for them to hide behind. These types of situations are most likely going to require coaching and/or mentoring of some sort.

Highlight potential constraints and possible supports you think might be factors and invite them to suggest possible supports and identify possible constraints. Explore each of them by asking questions and sharing your thoughts. Come to some agreement and consider how they need to be captured in the SMART format, e.g. under attainable, relevance, measurements, timeframes and roadmap.

Moving into Timeframe, invite the employee to suggest how they might go about achieving the objective. While you have done some serious preparation on this, again you want to avoid the feeling that the objective and the roadmap are faits accomplis. The preparation was to help you gain the resulting insights (i.e. clarification on outcomes, drivers, supports, assumptions, etc.) in your back pocket to guide questions and exploration rather than to direct and tell.

As you move towards the end of the discussion for each objective, review SMART and make sure it effectively captures all the discussion points. This is repeated until all the objectives, including the employee's proposed objectives, have been agreed and finalised.

INTROVERT OR EXTROVERT?

Before we finally leave this section, it's worth exploring Carl Jung's work on human preferences and how they could show up in this meeting. We already took a look at Intuition and Sensing in Chapter 3. In addition to that spectrum, there is the Introvert-Extrovert spectrum and Thinking-Feeling spectrum.

Those that demonstrate a preference for extroversion are more likely to express their thoughts and feelings and engage in dialogue during the meeting. The process of agreeing objectives in the actual meeting is more likely to happen with these people. The challenge with this group is likely to be around whether they have fully engaged in the objective, its outcomes and expectations.

For someone who demonstrates a preference for Extrovert Thinking, they typically want to get to the point as quickly as possible and move on. Their energy preference is go, go, go. They tend to like to action things so the need here is to slow them down long enough to properly map out a roadmap and have them recognise the potential constraints and barriers to success.

For someone who demonstrates a preference for Extrovert Feeling, they're likely to want to engage with the story but aren't overly taken with the detail. Drawing a picture of the outcome will resonate with them but, like their Extrovert Thinking cousins, they may not want to get too much into the detail because it bogs the story down. They will agree to the objective but may not have fully understood your expectations of it.

On the other hand, you may need to manage your expectations in relation to what will be agreed in the meeting with people who demonstrate a preference for introversion. Someone who demonstrates a preference for Introvert Thinking may need time to think through the suggested objectives and the roadmaps. This is by no means true of everyone who prefers Introvert Thinking, but it rings true of many of them. With people you suspect fall into this category, it may be best to break the objective setting into two meetings, allowing them the time to think through and consider the objectives between discussion and sign-off. This will increase their buy-in to the objectives. This can be kept loose, i.e. you keep the option of a follow-up meeting in your back pocket to pull out if and when you sense it is necessary.

Someone who demonstrates a preference for Introvert Feeling may or may not open up and tell you what they really think about these suggested objectives. Invest the time in asking questions and allowing the time for them to properly respond to ensure they really are buying into the objectives. Do *NOT* assume that if they are saying nothing it means that they buy into them. For many people with an Introvert Feeling preference, the relationship and feeling heard is very important to them. However, unlike someone with an extrovert preference, they are less likely to express their thoughts and feelings unless the environment is right for them. If they continuously feel they aren't being heard, the emotions are likely to spill out in other ways.

See Appendix 1: Carl Jung and Insights Discovery® Energy Preferences for further ideas on how to influence different energy preferences. As many people can pull from more than one energy preference, these are guidelines rather than absolutes.

While you're at it, you might want to think about your own energy preferences and compare them to each of your team member's energy preferences. Are they compatible or will you need to adjust your style in order to best influence them? If so, what adjustments will you need to make?

CONCLUDE THE OBJECTIVE-SETTING MEETING

The meeting conclusion should give a brief summary of what the meeting covered and also next steps. If the objectives need to be formally written up, agree who needs to do this and by when. While I've seen countless managers assume the responsibility for this, I always assign it to the employee as, after all, these are their objectives not mine. It feeds into the human sense of ownership. If they need to be signed off by both parties, as per your performance-management process, agree a final date and who's responsible for follow-up if it's not done.

I'm also very clear that these objectives are the employee's, not the manager's. I recommend that you stress that if the employee is running into issues, it's their responsibility to seek help. They should also be encouraged to keep their objectives somewhere in their line of sight and look at them on a weekly or bi-weekly basis to review how they're getting on. If there are sign-off meetings or regular monthly meetings required, or training, clarify where the responsibility lies to follow up, arrange, or schedule, if not already clearly agreed within each objective.

Having worked through all the different objectives and agreed the final list and what they look like, wrap up the meeting with words of motivation around what achieving these objectives will mean for the employee, the team, the organisation as a whole, and any other relevant third parties, such as the customer.

POST OBJECTIVE-SETTING MEETING

Ensure whoever was responsible for next steps follows up accordingly. If it has been agreed that the employee is responsible for actioning the next steps, follow up and ensure it is done, but don't take over, even if HR is hassling you for your outstanding documents.

CHAPTER SUMMARY

The objective-setting meeting is structured with:

- A formal opening, to explain the process and meeting outcomes/outputs
- A broad introduction to the objectives, linked back to performance feedback
- An exploration and agreement of each objective
- A formal meeting wrap-up and next steps

During the meeting, it's worthwhile considering the individual's energy preferences, e.g. Introvert Thinking, etc., and how best to meet their communication needs to increase the likelihood of their commitment to achieving the agreed objectives.

PROMPTS FOR YOU:

Go to Appendix 1 and review Figure 5: Energy Preferences on a Good Day and Bad Day and Figure 6: Influencing Each of the Colour Preferences. For each team member, using Figure 5, identify which colour energies most likely describe their preferences. Then using Figure 6, reflect on how people of that energy colour prefer to be communicated with and consider how you can adjust your approach to each person's preferences, to maximise the likelihood of each of them hearing your full message.

CONCLUSION

Developing competence in people is a core skill of management. This is equally true of a head of function developing their senior managers as it is of a team leader developing a junior member of staff. Being able to diagnose development needs and design an appropriate objective is core to the ability to develop other people's competence.

SMART is a very effective tool for designing effective goals. When using SMART between two people, the natural limitations of human communication can arise, reducing its effectiveness. Taking a literal interpretation of the different words of the SMART acronym allows both parties to assume different expectations and understanding of what has been agreed for an objective. This book demonstrates how to use SMART as a mechanism to have deeper conversations about the purpose of an objective, about how the outcomes relate to performance, about being realistic about the constraints and supports needed to succeed, and about how the employee might approach achieving the objective's outcomes.

As we saw, there are four different types of objectives—Role-Specific, Business-Aligned, Technical and Behavioural—some more tangible than others. The behavioural objectives can be very tricky both to articulate and develop. By continuously asking ourselves, "What's the business impact of this?" it can help us to depersonalise the behaviour and determine if it really is undermining the person's performance or if it's our own idiosyncratic issue to manage.

It takes time and effort to properly develop a competent and high-performing team. It takes time to properly reflect on and identify what a person's developmental needs are, and then it takes time to prepare for how to frame those developmental opportunities. It takes effort to properly support the team as they are implementing their objectives. However, all of this is part of the role of manager and, as managers, we reap the rewards through a competent team that we can rely on, freeing us up to work on projects that support the strategy or improve the effectiveness of the function or team. We also get to create opportunities for our team to become involved, further developing them.

As a manager, you can reap huge benefits from enabling your team and realising their potential, which further allows you to realise your own potential. However, in order to gain these benefits, several elements need to be in place so that you can tap into each member of your team's natural motivations, helping you all to succeed.

The first, and most crucial, element is having the right manager's performance mindset. Recognising and accepting that part of management is ensuring you have a competent team is the first step, genuinely believing that if everyone is performing to the right standard, everyone, including you as the manager, gains. If you believe this, everything else will flow.

The second element is having a clear view of the purpose of each role in the team, within the context of the job description and what it is designed to achieve, and the related knowledge, skills, and competencies required to succeed. Having an understanding of the level of complexity and how to move someone through learning the easier parts of the role, gradually building up to the more complex parts of the role, also falls into this element.

The third element is investing the time in planning for objective-setting meetings. Objectives that move the employee forward and tap into their own motivations are more likely to be achieved. Framing the objectives in terms of business impact and how they connect to the bigger picture, of the team, the client, or their own future career, helps you to do this. If they connect with their objectives, understand why these objectives should matter to them and tap into their motivations, the objective outcomes are more likely to be delivered, with the resultant increase in performance.

The ability to develop others is a very powerful tool and completely independent of HR's performance-management process. It is a core tool of management, and the more senior we get the more complex it is to develop direct reports. It is a lot easier to develop a financial accountant who produces tangible outputs than it is to develop a manager to manage their team or influence the executive team. The earlier a manager starts to learn and practice this skill, the easier it becomes and the more it stands to them as they progress up the ladder.

WHAT ARE MY NEXT STEPS?

Congratulations on finishing this book. I hope you enjoyed it and gained some ideas on how to approach your next round of objective-setting meetings. You might even decide to start making subtle changes today. If you're not sure what to do next, here is a range of Next Step ideas that you might find helpful:

INTRODUCING A NEW APPROACH TO YOUR TEAM

I'm hoping that, having read the book, you've identified some new tools and techniques that you are excited to apply during your next objective-setting cycle. If it is very different to your previous approach, you may need to introduce the new ideas to the team in advance of their next objective-setting meetings. A few suggestions on how to do this include:

- Answer the following question: What will you do differently during the next round of objective-setting meetings?
- Give a presentation to the team outlining the changes, explanations of new terminology, what they can expect and reasons for the changes
- One-to-one meetings to explain the changes, tailored to each individual's needs
- Check out Evolution Consulting's YouTube channel, Irial Evolution Consulting, and website, www.evolutionconsulting.ie, for suitable videos and courses that your team can sign up to

ADDITIONAL SUPPORT FOR YOU AS MANAGER

A book like this can only cover so many examples and so many types of cultures while, in reality, there are so many different situations that can arise. This may result in you feeling that you need more support tailored to your circumstances. Some ideas on how to obtain additional support include:

- Using the templates available to support this book to help you work through objective setting with your own team. If you haven't already, sign up here or go to www.evolutionconsulting.ie, to sign up and gain access.
- If you feel that you would benefit from a one-to-one coaching session with Irial, email her on irial.ofarrell@evolutionconsulting.ie or go to www.evolutionconsulting.ie and book a two-hour Performance Coaching session. The focus could be your Manager's Performance Mindset or working through a particular performance situation in preparation for the objective-setting meeting.
- If you'd like more examples of potential SMART behavioural objectives, Irial has developed a set of SMART Objectives cards. Each card outlines a specific developmental need and an example of how each element of a SMART objective could be set out. Buy them today by clicking on www.evolutionconsulting.ie or buy them on Amazon.com or Amazon.co.uk.
- If you'd like to explore your energy preferences and how they impact on your team, go to www.evolutionconsulting.ie and book a two-hour Insights Discovery® Assessment and Feedback session with Irial.

ADDITIONAL SUPPORT FOR YOUR ORGANISATION

You may be in a position to influence how objective setting is approached in your organisation. For example, you might work in HR or you might manage several managers or a function, or perhaps you're a member of the executive leadership team. Some ideas of how to introduce the approach across your organisation, as outlined in this book, include:

- Arrange a book club "lunch 'n' learn" meeting with a group of managers to discuss the book's contents and how it could be applied within your organisation. Depending on the audience, it may be wise to have a facilitator facilitate the discussion. As a Thank You for buying the book, use this discount code SMARTBulk20 to bulk-buy your books on www.evolutionconsulting.ie and get 20% off the retail price of three or more books.
- As a follow-on, arrange regular "Performance Discussion" meetings with this group to enable peer discussions on specific behavioural challenges and to support each other in diagnosing possible drivers and business impacts and how they might be framed. The Performance Issues Driver Analysis Template would be a good tool to guide such discussions.
- Contact Evolution Consulting to discuss creating a training and coaching program for your managers. This is a blended approach, combining videos, virtual workshops (in-person may also be possible), individual coaching sessions, complimentary copies of this book, articles and templates, and an online forum. It could be broadened out to include other aspects of Performance Management, such as Giving Effective Feedback, Developing High Performers, and Managing Underperformance. We can also work with you to incorporate your own performance-management process into the program.
- If you are considering redesigning your Performance-Management Process, contact Evolution Consulting to arrange a call to discuss how we can support you in incorporating the book's concepts into your new process and training.

Go to www.evolutionconsulting.ie and sign up, to keep up to date with Irial's blogs, podcasts and news on her forthcoming books. Topics will include:

- Giving Effective Feedback
- Developing High Performers
- Managing Chronic Underperformers
- Cascading Objectives
- Re-imagining Performance
- Developing Others' Problem-Solving Skills
- Management vs. Leadership
- Emotional Intelligence in Practice

APPENDIX 1

Carl Jung and Insights Discovery®'s Energy Preferences

Building on the work of Carl Jung, Insights Discovery® uses the following spectra to construct energy preferences, which are represented through colours: Cool Blue (Introvert Thinking), Fiery Red (Extrovert Thinking), Sunshine Yellow (Extrovert Feeling) and Earth Green (Introvert Feeling).

INTROVERSION VS. EXTROVERSION: Describes a person's preference concerning their interest in the world external to them (extroversion) and their own internal world (introversion). Extroverts typically are energised by being out in the world while introverts typically re-energise by time alone to reflect on their inner world.

INTUITION VS. SENSING: Describes a person's preference for taking in and absorbing information. Some prefer the more hands-on, practical approach (sensing) whereas others prefer to understand the concept (intuition).

THINKING VS. FEELING: Describes a person's preference for making decisions, ranging from using logical and detached analysis (Thinking) to an involved, subjective manner (Feeling).

Figure 5 indicates the types of words that best describe each colour energy when a person with that energy preference is on form and when they're having an off day; while Figure 6 provides tips on how best to influence each of the colour energy preferences.

Figure 5: Energy Preferences on a Good Day and Bad Day

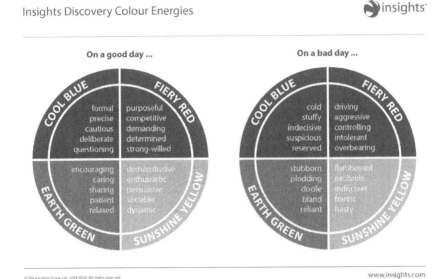

Figure 6: Influencing Each of the Energy Colour Preferences

REFERENCES

CHAPTER 3:

William Schiemann research link—14% of employees understand their company's strategy and direction—Performance Management: Putting Research into Action.

Andrew Lothian, Insights, Dundee, Scotland, 2006. Insights Discovery® Geographical Distribution. Insights Discovery® is a registered trademark owned by The Insights Group Limited.

CHAPTER 9:

Self-Determination Theory by Edward L Deci and Richard Ryan. For more information, go to: https://en.wikipedia.org/wiki/Self-determination_theory

GLOSSARY

ASSUMPTIONS	Thinking something is true or in place without questioning it or checking whether it is true or not, often without recognising we are making the assumption in the first place.
BELIEFS	Certain that something is true or exists, often without proof. Beliefs are often subconscious.
CARL JUNG	(1875–1961) Jung was a Swiss psychiatrist, who recognised how some people are energised by being in other people's company while others need alone time. He coined the terms *Introvert* and *Extrovert*. He also recognised Intuition vs. Sensing and Thinking vs. Feeling. For more information, go to https://en.wikipedia.org/wiki/Carl_Jung
COMPETENCE	Having the combination of knowledge, skills and application to be consistently able to do a task to the right standard.
CONFIRMATION BIAS	The tendency to seek out evidence that supports one's point of view.
EXPECTATIONS	Ways you think things will happen, e.g. how events will unfold, how a person will act, etc.

INSIGHTS DISCOVERY®   Assessment tool and model that captures the different energy preferences that arise from Carl Jung's work. Insights Discovery® is a registered trademark owned by The Insights Group Limited. For more information, go to www.insights.com

MYERS-BRIGGS   Assessment tool and model that captures the different energy preferences that arise from Carl Jung's work. This model also includes Judging vs. Perceiving. For more information, go to www.myersbriggs.org

NITTY GRITTY   Phrase that means *getting into the detail of something.*

OBJECTIVE DECISION CATEGORIES   Categories that describe the decision made, as to whether a manager will include an objective in the final set of objectives. Decision categories include: Must do, Optional, Hold Over and Reject.

OBJECTIVE DRIVERS   Clarifies what is driving the need for the objective. There can be more than one driver for a specific objective.

OBJECTIVE TYPES   The four broad categories are role-specific, business-aligned, technical competency and behavioural competency.

PERFORMANCE ASSESSMENT LEVELS   The four categories are Still Learning, Performance Issues, Good Performer and High Performer.

PERFORMANCE-MANAGEMENT PROCESS   The process that maps out the different stages associated with performance management along with all the related tasks. Typically includes setting objectives, monitoring performance, feedback, evaluation. It can also include succession planning, personal development plans, talent management, etc.

RECENCY BIAS	A tendency to recall recent events over events that happened further back in the past.
ROUND THE BEND	Phrase that means *driving someone crazy.*
SAP	SAP stands for Systems Applications and Products in Data Processing. It is the name of the Enterprise Resource Planning (ERP) software system sold by the company of the same name. For more information, go to www.sap.co.uk
SELF-DETERMINATION THEORY	A theory, by Deci and Ryan, that explains the different types of motivation that drive most people. It differentiates between natural motivations and how motivation might be influenced by environment.

ACKNOWLEDGEMENTS

I'd like to thank everyone who helped me with creating this book. To my reading crew—Fergal O'Farrell, Paul Clements, Nadine Chetty, Brendan O'Donovan, Yvonne McKenna and Brian McIvor—your feedback and ideas helped polish it. To Chandler Bolt, Lise Cartwright and everyone in the Self-Publishing School community, your help, enthusiasm and guidance were invaluable. To everyone who gave feedback on my cover options and to the people at 100Covers who designed it. To Keith, who has unending belief in me.

ABOUT THE AUTHOR

Irial lives in Dublin, Ireland, with her husband, three kids and two cats. She is fascinated with what makes people tick and she applies this through her work, working with companies and individuals to realise their potential. She loves reading (of course), learning new ideas and trying them out, travelling and quizzes. She really needs to join a quiz team some day soon.

Connect with her on: linkedin.com/in/irialofarrell
Follow her on: https://www.amazon.com/Irial-OFarrell/e/
B007GX1QIO
www.twitter.com/evolution_ary
https://www.facebook.com/
Evolution-Consulting-91352921868/
Like her books on: https://www.facebook.com/Irial-OFarrell-Books

COPYRIGHT PERMISSIONS

Thanks to The Insights Group Limited, for their kind permission for using their Insights Discovery® model, analysis data and for reproducing their images in Figure 5: Energy Preferences on a Good Day and Bad Day and Figure 6: Influencing Each of the Energy Colour Preferences.

ONE FINAL OBJECTIVE

Want to help ?

Did you know that only 1 in 100 readers leave a review?

If you found this book beneficial, it would be great if you could share your thoughts about it with other people who might also benefit. Book readers rely on reviews to decide which books to buy. I would really appreciate if you took one minute to rate and review this book on your eReader, Amazon, or other chosen platform.

Thank you for taking the time.

Printed in Great Britain
by Amazon